FRONT LINE AVENGER SQUADRONS
of the FAA

R.G. Fletcher

Published in Great Britain by
R.G.Fletcher,
8, Woodland Place,
Great Barton,
BURY St. EDMUNDS,
Suffolk,
IP31 2TG

© 1995 R.G.Fletcher

ISBN 0-9518877-1-8

British Library Cataloguing-in-Publication Data.
A catalogue record of this book is available from the British Library.

Designed and set by
ARIOMA,
Gloucester House, High Street,
BORTH, Dyfed, SY24 5HZ
Tel/Fax (01970) 871296

Printed by
Cambrian Printers,
Llanbadern Road,
ABERYSTWYTH,
Dyfed, SY23 3TN

Cover design by ARIOMA. Photograph *FAA Museum*

DEDICATION

To the memory of Fleet Air Arm aircrew who lost their lives during World War Two, remembering particularly the nine members shot down at Palembang, captured by the Japanese and brutally executed, amongst which were my former pilot and observer:

Lt. (A) K.M. Burrenston RNVR
S/Lt. (A) W.E. Lintern RNVR

"NONE OF US SHOULD FORGET"

U.K. BASES MENTIONED IN TEXT

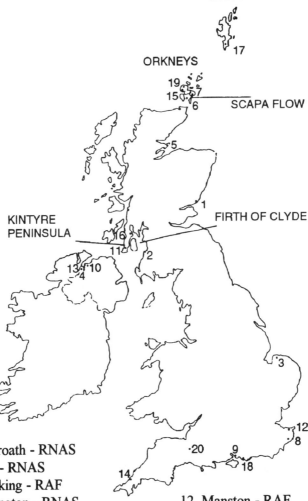

SHETLANDS

ORKNEYS

SCAPA FLOW

KINTYRE PENINSULA

FIRTH OF CLYDE

1. Arbroath - RNAS
2. Ayr - RNAS
3. Docking - RAF
4. Eglington - RNAS
5. Fearn - RNAS
6. Grimsetter - RNAS
7. Hatston - RNAS
8. Hawkinge - RAF
9. Lee-on-Solent - RNAS
10. Limavady - RAF
11. Macrihanish - RNAS

12. Manston - RAF
13. Maydown - RNAS
14. Perranporth - RAF
15. Skeabrae - RAF
16. Skipness - WRNS
17. Sumburgh - RAF
18. Thorney Island - RAF
19. Twatt - RNAS
20. Yeovilton - RNAS

CONTENTS

ILLUSTRATIONS

Life on *Indefatigable* with the BPF, 1945 as seen by Chuck Sage.

Photographic section

MAPS

Cover Pictures

ACKNOWLEDGEMENTS

I wish to record my appreciation of the assistance which I have received in the preparation of this book, particularly from the following:

Mrs. Valerie Bain;   G.E. Hearn;   A.R. Howes;

R.D. Pankhurst;   J.C. Medcalf;   Cdr. J.W. Powell, RN;

J. Richardson;   M.D. Richardson;   Mrs. Iris Sage;

H.J.C. Spencer;   W. Taylor.

I also wish to thank those contemporaries of mine who have contributed accounts of their experiences for inclusion in the book. A list of these is given elsewhere.

Finally, I have to thank my good friend Vernon Ball who has yet again given me his support and encouragement throughout the project while Moira and Patrick Smith, of Arioma, have supplied the professional expertise and advice to produce the book.

FOREWORD

Few books have been written by Telegraphist Air Gunners of the Fleet Air Arm about their experiences and none, as I am aware, of their experiences in all front-line Avenger squadrons in World War Two. This book gives a detailed description of day-to-day life for a TAG on an Avenger squadron from forming up to its disbanding. Into the outline history of squadrons, the author has introduced the personal experiences of over twenty of his contemporaries thus covering the whole range of Avenger operations. Every aspect of their duties is described and explained in a manner that makes the reader feel present at the event whether it be a practice torpedo attack, a carrier landing or the attack on Palembang. The reason for this realism is that these are the men who were there and it shows.

The book is a valuable contribution to the chronicles of FAA aircrew in World War Two while being eminently readable.

Captain W.J. Flindell, FRAeS, RN,
Director, The Fleet Air Arm Museum.

FRONT LINE AVENGER SQUADRONS OF THE FAA DURING WORLD WAR TWO

SQUADRON	FORMED	DISBANDED
820	1/10/44	16/03/46
828	1/02/45	3/06/46
832	1/01/43	21/02/45
845	1/02/43	7/10/45
846	1/04/43	22/09/45
848	1/06/43	31/10/45
849	1/08/43	31/10/45
850	1/09/43	24/12/44
851	1/10/43	07/10/45
852	1/11/43	17/10/44
853	1/12/43	30/05/45
854	1/01/44	8/12/45
855	1/02/44	19/10/44
856	1/03/44	15/06/45
857	1/04/44	30/11/45

INTRODUCTION

It was early in December, 1942, when I first heard of the Avenger. Having just been awarded my wings as a Telegraphist Air Gunner, I was at the Fleet Air Arm base at Lee-on-Solent awaiting draft to a squadron and was somewhat anxious to know what my first operational posting would be. With others from my Course I would eagerly listen to the many rumours which circulated concerning the possible destinations to which we might be sent. Although we had been given the opportunity to register a preference for the type of squadron which we would wish to join, it was generally accepted that this gesture on the part of the establishment was of little practical effect. Hence our great interest in any news, however dubious its source, which might indicate the possible locations to which we could be drafted.

On this particular morning, as I emerged from the NAAFI canteen, with a number of other TAGs, one of them started to relate the latest rumour about the formation of a new squadron which would be equipped with an aircraft called the Avenger. According to him, the plane, to be supplied by the USA, as part of their lend lease programme, had enclosed cabins, a speed of around 250 mph and was capable of carrying a bomb load of a ton. Compared with the aircraft in current use with the FAA, namely the Swordfish and Albacore, these specification details, even allowing for the inevitable exaggeration, were incredible. However, what really captured my attention was the assertion that the plane had a power-operated gun turret; to an air-gunner trained on a single Lewis or Vickers, such a statement seemed unbelievable. But then came the sting in the tail when the TAG, continuing his description of the turret, said that, owing to its compactness, it would only accommodate TAGs under 5ft.5ins in height. As I would exceed that requirement by 6 ins, my hopes for such a draft were quickly extinguished and my thoughts turned to the more likely options available little knowing that my fate had already been decided.

Next morning, I received my drafting instructions to report to HMS Condor at Arbroath, there, to join the Tarmac Party at the No.2 Observer School. At the time, it seemed a great let-down to be assigned to ground duties having just spent almost a year qualifying as a member of flying crew; such was the vanity of youth! For two weeks, I struggled to carry out my duties realising that I was not quite as competent as I had believed when facing the practicalities of everyday life on the tarmac. Then, a few days later, I was sent on a week's leave prior to joining a new squadron, forming up at Lee-on-Solent, which was to be equipped with the new TBF aircraft, the Avenger. So it was that, on 1st January, 1943, I joined 845 Avenger squadron with which I served for nearly two and a half years.

I shall always remember my first sight of it when, having arrived at the USNAS at Quonset Point in the evening, I and a few other TAGs slipped into the nearby hangar. There they stood with wings folded looking like gigantic insects in metamorphosis waiting for their wings to spread before they could get airborne. In the pools of shadow cast by the hangar lights, the Avengers huge bulk fronted by the immense 13 foot propeller was an awesome sight to an impressionable teenager who was going to fly in them. My subsequent experience of flying in Avengers left me with an abiding respect for this great plane and, hence, a deep interest in the exploits of all the Avenger squadrons.

In the following chapters, I have attempted, at this late stage on the fiftieth anniversary of the end of the war with Japan, to describe the Avenger's wartime role as experienced, by the Telegraphist Air Gunner. The story is restricted to the 15 front-line squadrons which were formed, or were re-equipped, as Avenger squadrons and shows how the Avenger undertook differing roles in the various theatres of the war. It does not purport to be a detailed history of the squadrons although an outline of the main events of each, from forming-up to disbandment, has been included as a background to the TAG experiences recounted.

The narration of events in respect of a number of squadrons existing contemporaneously raises certain problems in relation to maintaining chronological coherence. Squadrons existed for differing periods, from as little as eight months to as much as thirty-two months, but all during a three year period. It follows that to keep strict chronological order is impossible without rendering the narrative virtually meaningless. Consequently, it has been necessary to abandon any attempt to maintain chronological sequence for the book as a whole while maintaining it for each individual squadron.

The number of TAGs serving on the 15 squadrons at some time during their existence was probably of the order of 500 and yet, after 50 years, it has been possible to get over 20 of these to contribute their experience which cover all but one of the squadrons. This remarkable achievement has, in great part, been due to the existence of the Telegraphist Air Gunners Association to which most of the contributors belong.

As would be expected, many features of squadron life were common to all; the process of forming-up, the training exercises, the working-up procedures, and even the airfields and ships served on were often the same. Accordingly, it would be pointless to repeat these details for all squadrons and so such matters will, in general, be detailed for one squadron only. For personal reasons, I have chosen 845 but there are other considerations for the choice, it was the first Avenger squadron to be formed and also the longest serving.

Finally, it is perhaps pertinent to mention two matters which affected the outlook of a TAG as a member of the Avenger's three-man crew. First, the composition of the crew; with very few exceptions, all pilots and observers were commissioned officers while TAGs were ratings. Because of this difference in rank, in the Royal Navy at least, social contacts between them were rarely made outside of duty hours. Of course, there was a greater degree of friendliness in some crews than in others but, in general, there was a definite feeling of "them and us". In most instances, this state of affairs was accepted and caused no resentment but in some hostility was engendered. Perhaps it was an attempt to reduce any such animosity which prompted the Captain of *Indefatigable*, in 1945, to grant permission for rating aircrew to mess in the Wardroom on days of operational flying. Whether that was appreciated by both ratings and officers is debatable but, at least, it was an unprecedented move on the Captain's part. The second matter, which involves both observer and TAG, is that of being a back-seat member of the crew. As such, he is a hostage to fortune, albeit the fortune of the pilot, as it is upon the pilot's actions that those in the back depend. Although their assistance may be essential to the pilot, in such things as navigation, communication, or gunnery defence, their best efforts would be futile without the pilot; in effect, he is the end-player. This fact soon becomes apparent to a back-seat man and unless he has confidence in his pilot's abilities then flying becomes a most nerve-racking experience. A further factor with which the Avenger TAG had to contend was his position in the gun-turret where, facing backward like a passenger on a train with his back to the engine, he was always seeing what had gone before rather than what was to come, unlike the pilot. However, on some occasions, he might be faced by fate overtaking him in the form of an enemy fighter. In the turret, as in the rear cockpit, the TAG was remote from his other crewmen and sometimes it could feel very lonely.

PROFILE OF THE AVENGER

The first prototype of the Grumman Avenger flew in August, 1941, and the first production models were delivered early in 1942. It was designed as a torpedo-bomber to replace the Douglas Devastator and the first operational deployment of the new plane was in June at the Battle of Midway where it had a most inauspicious start. Of the six planes which set out to attack the Japanese carrier force only one returned and that badly damaged. However, despite this initial setback, the Avenger had, by the beginning of 1943, established itself as a capable and reliable combat plane.

One Avenger was received in the UK for testing and the first deliveries of Tarpon Is were made to the Fleet Air Arm in the USA at the start of 1943. The unimaginative name of Tarpon had been designated by the Admiralty but fortunately this was abandoned in January, 1944, for the more emotive name of Avenger. Around 400 of this version were supplied until 1944 when Avenger IIs entered service manufactured by the Eastern Aircraft Division of General Motors who supplied 334 of the mark followed by 192 of their Avenger IIIs late in the war.

The 900 plus aircraft delivered to the FAA were used to equip 15 front-line squadrons and over 20 second-line units; the latter having only a part of their complement as Avengers. Although designed primarily as a torpedo-bomber and used so by the US Navy Air Service, the Avenger was rarely deployed with torpedoes in the FAA where it served mainly as a bomber with bombs, mines and depth charges or as a strike aircraft with rocket projectiles.

The Avenger soon earned the confidence of its crews because of

5

its reliability, performance, and innate sturdiness. The last characteristic being particularly important when ditching as it rarely broke up on impact and tended to remain afloat sufficiently long to allow the crew members to get out of the aircraft. Even with dead stick landings on land, the stoutness of the construction often protected the crew when collision with obstacles such as fences, hedges, poles etc. proved unavoidable.

The Avenger was probably the heaviest single-engined combat plane to be built and its relative lack of manoeuvrability was to be expected. On the other hand, it was very stable in flight and this stability aided by the huge sting-type arrester hook made landing on a carrier as easy as such a difficult operation could ever be. In flight, it had few vices but the stall could occur suddenly and without warning and the Pilot's Notes did warn against putting the aircraft into a spin intentionally. The diving speed with a full load was restricted officially to 285 knots and at this speed the pull-out was a strenuous affair.

The aircraft was a mid-wing monoplane of all-metal, stressed-skin construction and had accommodation for three crew members. Behind the pilot's cockpit, there was a central glasshouse compartment given over to the accommodation of radio and other equipment. Then came the Browning 0.5-in gun turret and astern of this the lower cabin, occupying the whole of the fuselage behind the bomb-bay, entered by a door aft of the starboard wing. Inside, there was a folding bench-type seat facing forward opposite the radio and radar sets while below these there was a Perspex panel which, when the bomb bay doors were open, provided a downwards view for the bombardier as used by the USNAS. Above the radio was the access door to the turret and, on the right there was space to crawl into the central glasshouse. To the rear of the seat, was the ventral gun position, equipped with a Browning 0.3-in firing aft. The cabin was poorly lit, having only one Perspex blister and a smaller window on each side although some daylight did filter down via the turret. The use of this lower cabin by the observer and TAG proved to be unsatisfactory for the former as visibility was poor and the use of navigational charts and instruments while sharing the bench seat with the TAG was not conducive to effective work or amicable relationships.

Consequently, by transferring equipment from the central glasshouse compartment, it was possible to provide the observer with a position which had excellent visibility and better facilities for his navigational duties. It also left the rear cabin for the exclusive use of the TAG, apart from the very occasional passenger. With this change, the ventral gun position was, in some squadrons, considered dispensable and removed.

The communications equipment installed in the Avenger was of high quality and superb in performance. The TAG had MF/HF radio transmitter and receiver with plug-in coil units for each frequency range connected to an HF fixed aerial but with a trailing aerial, for MF, operated from the lower cabin. However, this equipment was replaced later in 1943 with even more advanced models which had automatic selection of 10 frequencies on the transmitter and waveband switching on the receiver; these innovations eliminated the need for the plug-in coils on both.

The observer had ASB radar, an American version of British ASV, which was linked to two remote-controlled aerials located one under each mainplane.

The pilot had a radio altimeter which was very sophisticated for that period and would have been particularly useful for torpedo operations. He also had control of a VHF transmitter/receiver with 4 set frequencies; as this operated on a "line of sight" principle it could be used under conditions of radio silence.

Also available to the crew was a homing receiver, operating on VHF, which could be used to obtain the course to fly for a particular home base, be that ship or landbase. There were plug-in boxes around the aircraft, linked to the main radio receiver, which provided inter-communication between crew members. Finally, the plane was fitted with an IFF system, an American version of British equipment, which triggered off a coded response to a signal transmitted by the home base thereby identifying whether friend or foe.

The bulkiness of the airframe, a characteristic of the Grumman carrier aircraft, was accentuated by the provision of a capacious internal bomb bay. This was able to house a 22-in torpedo, or four 500-lb. bombs or their equivalent in mines and depth charges, alternatively a long-range fuel tank could be fitted. Externally, rocket projectiles could be carried under the wings. In addition to these attack capabilities, the plane was well equipped for self-defence with its turret and ventral gun positions and a 0.3-in gun, in the engine cowling, provided for the pilot; this last gun was replaced by two 0.5-in Brownings, one in each wing.

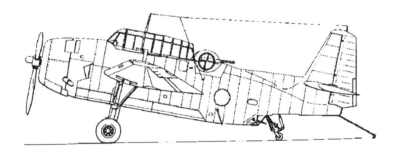

TECHNICAL SPECIFICATION - MARK I & II

Description   A three-seat, mid-wing monoplane, carrier borne, of all-metal, stressed-skin construction used for torpedo, bombing, mine-laying, anti-submarine and reconnaissance operations.

Manufacturers Grumman Aircraft Engineering Corporation, Bethpage, New York. Also sub-contracted to General Motors Eastern Aircraft Division, Trenton, New Jersey.

Power Plant   Wright Cyclone 14 cylinder, radial engine of 1750 hp.

Dimensions   Wing span 54ft 2ins, folded 19ft., length 40ft.

Weight   Empty 10,600 1b, loaded 16,400 1b, with wing tanks 17,350 1b.

Performance   Maximum speed 230 knots, cruising 160 knots, range 1100 miles, with no bombs & extra fuel 2000 miles, service ceiling 21,500ft.

Armament   2 fixed 0.05-in machine-guns in wings, 0.30-in in ventral position, and 0.50-in in dorsal turret. Internal bomb-bay for one 22-in torpedo, or four 500 1b bombs, or equivalent mines and depth charges. Eight rocket projectiles under wings

Note   The Mark III Avenger was equipped with a slightly more powerful version of the same engine which gave marginal improvements in performance. Although a number were delivered to the FAA, few saw active service in the war.

Stand by to receive one TBF

FORMATION OF SQUADRONS

Of the fifteen front-line Avenger squadrons, only twelve of them were newly-formed. The first of these was 845, which formed at USNAS Quonset Point, Rhode Island, on 1st February, 1943, followed by 846 on 1st April, 848 on 1st June, and 849 on 1st August. The remaining eight were formed at USNAS Squantum, Massachusetts, starting with 850 on 1st September and then at monthly intervals until 1st April, 1944, when 857 was formed. The other three were existing squadrons which were re-equipped with Avengers; they included 832 in January, 1943, 820 in October, 1944, and 828 in February, 1945. The last two squadrons each had a complement of 21 aircraft, with the rest having 12, some of these were later reduced to 9 with a sub-flight of Wildcat fighters.

The forming-up process involved the crews, both air and ground, learning the theoretical and practical aspects of their new equipment, practising with that equipment to acquire the requisite individual levels of competence, and then training together as a squadron to achieve the basic operating effectiveness for front line service. After this would come the specialised training to meet the specific requirements called for by the demands of the operational role planned for each squadron:

The average time allowed for forming a new squadron was about three months but in the case of those squadrons re-equipping this was reduced to about two months. The training to achieve basic squadron effectiveness was similar for all squadrons and is exemplified by that for 845, which was the first to be formed.

After forming up, came, for front-line squadrons, the process of working up which was, by necessity, a continuing process throughout its existence. There was a constant need to meet the requirements of change, whether in ships, equipment, crews, type of operation or theatre of war which meant practice, practice, practice. So, during the intervals between operations, the emphasis was on working-up to maintain peak efficiency in preparation for whatever demands might be made.

Having achieved both technical and practical effectiveness in their new aircraft and associated equipment, the squadrons had now to gain their operational competence by working with that naval unit for which purpose they had been formed - the aircraft carrier. Although, during the war, several Avenger squadrons operated against the enemy from land bases, most did so from a carrier. All the 13 squadrons which trained in the US returned on carriers, in some cases as passengers, in others as the resident squadron. In the latter cases, the squadron was faced with a period of working-up, in most instances, with a ship which had little experience of operating with a squadron, so there was much to learn on both sides.

* * * *

Owing to the heavy losses sustained by its carrier force in the first eleven months of the war with Japan, the US Navy had only two large carriers in service by the end of October, 1942. An appeal to the British Government for the loan of a fleet carrier could not be met at the time as Operation TORCH, the landing in North Africa, was imminent and the invasion was to be supported by seven British carriers, including the two fleet carriers *Formidable* and *Victorious*. However, when the airfields ashore had been secured, the *Victorious* was released for service with the US Navy. 832 Squadron, which had served on *Victorious* since forming up in April, 1941, was reformed at RNAS Crail before re-embarking in December, 1942; the ship sailed for Norfolk, Virginia, a few days before Christmas. After a rough passage, during which the ship was diverted to Bermuda for shelter from the storm, *Victorious* arrived at Norfolk on 1st January. There the squadron went ashore to the USNAS for a period of intensive training on the their new aircraft, the USN TBF-1

Avenger.

When the squadron reformed, there were changes in aircrew, and of the TAG complement six were members of TAG 35 Course, who had only recently gained their wings. On 10th January, only ten days into their squadron training, one of their number was killed in a tragic accident. Leading Airman Jock McEvoy died of injuries sustained when an Avenger crashed into a hangar as he was performing the daily inspection of the radio equipment in the lower cabin. At the time, the engine of the aircraft was being run up by the air mechanic when it jumped the chocks and hit the nearby hangar wall.

Squadron training continued until the end of the month, while in the meantime, the *Victorious* was in the Navy Yard having the gun-sponsons removed in preparation for passage through the Panama Canal. At that time, it was the widest ship to attempt the passage, having only a foot or so clearance on either side in the locks; hence the need for the removal of the projecting sponsons. With the ship ready for sailing, the squadron re-embarked and *Victorious* proceeded south to the Canal and, once through, the sponsons were replaced before starting on its voyage across the Pacific. During passage, the usual anti-submarine patrols were flown but on February 28th things did not go as usual. An Avenger, returning from patrol, hooked an arrester wire at an angle which caused it to veer to port and come to rest partly hanging over the side. In doing so, it burst into flames and although all three crew members were rescued, the pilot and TAG were badly burned. George Smith, another TAG, was in the Sick Bay at the time, suffering from Dengue fever, and recalls Leading Airman W.F. Lovell, MID, being put in a nearby berth, but he unfortunately died from his injuries.

The *Victorious* reached Pearl Harbour in early March when 832 flew ashore to USNAS Luke Field where they continued their working-up. During this time, the TAGs attended the Kaneohe Bay Gunnery School for two weeks training on the Avenger's power-operated turret gun. Returning to Luke Field, training continued with air-firing exercises for the TAGs. Then, in the second week of May, the squadron went aboard *Victorious* which sailed to join USS

Saratoga, the fleet carrier, at Noumea, New Caledonia. For 832, their working-up would be subject to operational demands; they would be learning the job while doing it!

At the base at Noumea, *Victorious* joined Task Group 36.3 including the American carrier *Saratoga*, and battleships *Indiana* and *Massachusetts*. Their first operations were in support of the American landings on New Georgia, in the British Solomon Islands, by providing air cover and attacking Japanese coastal positions. Then, at the end of June, 832 went aboard *Saratoga* to join the USN Avenger squadrons while the USN fighter squadrons embarked on *Victorious*. For the next month, the Task Group operated in the Coral Sea and supported further landings in the Solomons. At that time, after the great carrier battles of 1942, the Japanese fleet was replacing its losses in ships and aircrew and was in no fit state to oppose the American carrier forces. The FAA were thus denied the opportunity of taking part in an air battle between carriers. TAG, George Smith, recalls with pleasure his service on *Saratoga*, the quarters with bunk beds, the good food, the laundry facilities, the ice-cream bars, the entertainment and the uniform. As regards the last item, they had been kitted out in Hawaii with the khaki shirts and trousers of the US Navy - the British style shorts were not approved of by the Americans. It was one of the rare occasions that RN aircraft had operated from a USN carrier.

Early in August, the *Victorious* left the Task Group and headed for home, calling first at Hawaii, then San Diego, before passing through the Panama Canal, and finally Norfolk, Virginia. It arrived Greenock late September, nine months and many thousands of miles since departing from there.

* * * *

845 squadron personnel were brought together at Lee-on-Solent during the first half of January, 1943, and of the 12 TAGs, several were pre-war entries, others had been TAGs for a year or two, and the remaining four of us had only recently finished our training. The senior TAG was Petty Officer Tom Woolmer, some ten years older

than most of us, experienced, competent and respected throughout the squadron. Overall, the squadron had been given an above-average complement of TAGs.

For our passage to New York, we went aboard HMT *Queen Elizabeth,* departing January, 19th and arriving on the 25th. The voyage was uneventful apart from one of the worst Atlantic storms for some years and for those of the squadron going to sea for the first time it was a rough introduction. Personally, my taste for Hershey chocolate bars, purchased from the ship's shop before sailing, did not survive the trip! Disembarking on the 26th, the squadron moved to Astbury Park, New Jersey, a naval transit camp consisting of two hotels where we stayed for three days.

The squadron arrived at USNAS Quonset Point at the end of January, 1943, where the weather was bright but extremely cold with 30 degrees of frost or more. The normal naval uniform was not designed for such temperatures and in consequence we felt the cold badly although TAGs were not averse to wearing their flying clothing, such as boots and Irvine jackets for warmth, even when going on leave from the camp. The quarters were warm and comfortable, despite the outside temperatures, and the separate blocks were joined by enclosed passageways making it possible to walk from the quarters to the mess hall without venturing outside. The food served was plentiful and, in some cases, somewhat unusual to British palates which had become accustomed to the austerity diets of wartime Britain. One feature of the mess hall which I recall particularly well was the design of the dining-tables, which were strongly built with eight legs to each of which was attached a swivel seat. The table would accommodate up to eight diners, but there was a need to balance the weight on either side, otherwise it would tip up. In our first days, no doubt the US servicemen could recognise newcomers, and if they were on one side of the table then, having finished their meal, they might all vacate their seats at the same time. The result was a tray full of food in the laps of the persons remaining. However, one such experience was sufficient to alert the senses to avoid any future occurrences.

The squadron soon settled down to their new surroundings and the training programme started in earnest. For the first week, TAGs had to attend instruction upon their new equipment both radios and guns both of which were entirely unknown to them. The radio sets were far more sophisticated than those installed in FAA aircraft but the greatest change was the use of radio-telephony (R/T) in place of morse. Although, the morse key would continue to be used on medium frequencies for long distance communication, for all intents and purposes' voice communication would be used for most of the time while airborne. This did not help the TAG to maintain his competence in the sending and receiving of morse which had been the main element of his training. However, the advantages of speech communication far outweighed any apparent disadvantages; it was only when the TAG found himself put on a W/T watch on a ship that his lack of proficiency became apparent. It was particularly the case with TAGs, such as myself, who coming straight off Course found themselves using R/T and had no real opportunity to develop their skills in W/T. Whether that deficiency was of consequence is debatable since, ironically, most operational duties were carried out in strict radio silence.

To improve our shooting ability, all TAGs underwent a course in skeet shooting, the American equivalent of clay pigeon shooting, and as this took place outdoors, the intense cold made the jarring of the double-barrelled shotgun against the cheek most painful. Nevertheless, we survived and by the end of the course most were able to score 28 hits out of 30. It was obviously thought that the skill involved in skeet shooting, the ability to judge the aim-off for targets approaching from different directions, could be transferred to firing a turret-gun at an enemy fighter; certainly the principle is the same.

With a ceiling of over 20,000 feet, the Avenger was equipped with oxygen masks and, to acquaint crews with their use, we received training from the Americans, making use of their decompression chamber. In groups of about a dozen, we were locked in the chamber and the atmospheric pressure was reduced, in stages, to the equivalent of 10,000 feet and 20,000 feet; the intention of the training was to make one aware of the symptoms of lack of oxygen. To this end, each member of the crew was given a clerical test to perform at ground level, and at 10,000 feet with no oxygen and then at 20,000 feet with oxygen. For a normal person, the test would show a lower mark for the test taken at 10,000 feet without oxygen whereas the marks for the other two tests would be around the same. Hence the lack of oxygen would be shown to have affected the mental processes of the individuals without them being conscious of the fact; for aircrew a danger to avoid. With the tests completed, we handed in our tests for assessment on leaving the chamber and, the next day, our individual assessment marks were received at the squadron office. To my embarrassment, I had achieved higher marks for my test without oxygen than for the two with it. Nothing was said about this anomaly so I decided to let sleeping dogs lie!

Flying training began in early February and for me the first flight was in Avenger FN750 which was the first serial number of the initial batch of true FAA Avengers; it was logged as a familiarisation trip. For the rest of the month, flying was devoted to pilot training with formation flying and practice approaches from 10,000 feet to sea-level. On one of the latter, I record that the aircraft reached a speed of 330 knots in the dive; I still recall the pilot telling me of his achievement, after we had landed. It was sobering to hear months later, that during a major inspection, cracks were found in the wings of some of our aircraft. From then on, the advice in the pilot's handbook against exceeding 300 knots was put into effect, with the maximum speed when fully loaded being restricted to 285 knots.

In March, the flying consisted mainly of formation flying and simulated torpedo attacks both by day and by night. On one occasion the squadron was aloft for 4 hours 10 minutes, trying in vain to find the target of their practice attack. By now, the TAGs were operating the R/T as of the manner born and using the turret against feint attacks by other Avengers

By April, individual crews had been settled, my pilot being S/Lt. K.M. Burrenston and my observer S/Lt. W.E. Lintern. We were now flying sometimes twice a day, the emphasis being on practice torpedo attacks by day and night; targets were often US warships, and dummy torpedoes were sometimes dropped. Similarly, dive bombing attacks were made on targets using 250lb dummy bombs and there was the first firing of the turret-guns and the pilots' front guns at smoke floats dropped in the sea. I had two unusual trips during the month, one was a visit to the Hamilton Standard Propellers factory at Hartford, Connecticut, and the other a routine night navigation exercise which had to be abandoned when my radio transmitter burst into flames. I still recall the anxious voice of my pilot saying, over the intercom, "I can smell burning," and he was right. Luckily, the fire was confined to the set and was soon extinguished but at night, a few hundred miles out to sea and with the transmitter useless, the experience was a little unnerving.

May, which proved to be our last month at Quonset, was given over almost entirely to turret-gun firing practice. The target drogues were towed by Avengers, crews taking turns for the task, which I found a little unnerving with the thought of those 0.5 Brownings being sprayed in our direction. My confidence was not increased by the knowledge that the results of the exercises showed a low level of hits on the target. In that case, where were all those bullets going! Compared with the results which I achieved on my TAG Course, where the percentage of hits was always in double figures, my efforts in the turret showed only one 10% strike and even included a nil%. Even though the two sets of results were not strictly comparable, as the range, rate of fire, and calibre of the Browning and Vickers were vastly different, the results were disconcerting to me, never mind my crew. However, I was not alone in my low scoring rate and eventually other factors came to light which helped to explain the poor results.

During our stay in the US, we enjoyed a great deal of hospitality from American families, and some members of the squadron were so well ensconced that they often spent nights ashore, duties permitting. The squadron also fielded rugby and hockey teams for games against other FAA units on the station. Harvard University, who had a rugby team at that time, offered the FAA a match at their campus and the team were entertained royally over the weekend. I had declined an invitation to join the team but regretted my decision after hearing of the hospitality received. Then, a few weeks later, the FAA were asked to provide a few players to play for Harvard itself and this time I eagerly accepted the invitation. However, the flying programme that particular weekend precluded my going and so my ambition to have played for Harvard was thwarted - a missed opportunity which I regret to this day.

On May 28th, after nearly four months working-up, the squadron left Quonset bound for the USN base at Norfolk, Virginia, where we were to embark on *Chaser*, which was to be the first British escort carrier to have an Avenger squadron aboard. During the four months, I had put in 86 hours flying time, comprising 64 flights, which represented about 1,000 hours for the squadron as a whole. Having joined the squadron as a novice, I now felt confident of performing my duties as a TAG and, enjoying good relations with my crew, I found flying in Avengers exhilarating. The squadron, which had started as a collection of individual servicemen of varying age, rank, experience and specialisation, had now acquired an incorporeal entity of its own to which we had all contributed. A new squadron had been born and had now to develop its own traditions of service.

On 27th May, 845 Squadron pilots flew to Norfolk, Virginia, for two days deck landing trials on USS *Charger*, while the rest of the squadron personnel travelled by train, starting out at 1400 on 28th.

We had reserved compartments with our own dining car and I found the 600 mile journey fascinating. In the evening, the open coaches were made up into sleeping compartments and we retired in style. I still remember waking during the night, when the train stopped at the main stations, and looking out to see such names as Philadelphia, Baltimore, and Washington; it all seemed like a dream to a teenager who had not travelled abroad before this American visit. We left the train at 0700 and boarded a ferry for a three hour journey to Norfolk, where we took a tram to the US Naval base and finally arrived at our destination, *Chaser*. I was not impressed by what I saw from the dockside - a forbidding grey hulk.

The *Chaser* was one of the Attacker Class escort carriers, commissioned in the previous month. It was built by Ingalls, with a displacement of 14,400 tons fully laden, a flight deck 440 feet by 82 feet, speed of 18 knots, aircraft operational capacity of 15 to 20, and a ship's complement of 650. Unlike British ships in which the traditional ways of the Royal Navy held sway, the CVE was equipped to American standards. Meals were served and eaten in a central dining area, in the manner of a cafeteria, with the canteen, run by the NAAFI, open during the meal times. The ratings' sleeping quarters were located below the hangar deck and were equipped with three-level bunks, arranged in units of six, separated by narrow gangways. Rows of steel lockers were provided for the storage of personal belongings and there was a small area with tables and chairs for recreational purposes. The lighting and ventilation systems did nothing to improve what was a dreary, depressing, and claustrophobic place to spend your free time. Fortunately, there was an aircrew Ready Room, located just below the flight deck on the port side, fitted with comfortable armchairs and air conditioning equipment. As TAGs, we were entitled to use the Ready Room and tended to spend a large amount of our time in there. In the hot weather, the air conditioning was a real boon, but it was often out of order, for reasons which I never learned. The ship was also equipped with a laundry and when operated this also was of great benefit to ratings.

When the squadron boarded the *Chaser*, I had never served on a Royal Navy warship before and so I accepted the living arrangements on board as standard for the RN generally. It was not until a year later when I served on *Illustrious*, where traditional messing arrangements were in force, that I realised the difference between the two systems. The traditional method meant that the individual mess-deck was used for eating, sleeping, and off-duty activities. The food was collected by mess cooks from the central galley and served on the mess-tables, over which, at night, the individual hammocks would be slung for sleeping. I for one found such living arrangements anathema after experiencing those on the American CVEs which, initially, I thought were awful.

On 31st May, *Chaser* put to sea for trials in Chesapeake Bay; it was a case of a new squadron needing carrier experience on a new ship whose ship's company had to learn how to operate aircraft. For the next three weeks the squadron carried out exercises, mainly dummy torpedo attacks, from the ship, which put into port every few days for modifications or repairs. For some reason, which I have long forgotten, my first flight from the ship, an RDF calibration exercise, was not with my usual crew. The pilot for my first deck landing was S/Lt.(A) R. Halliday, who was later to have a distinguished naval career, eventually retiring as a Vice Admiral. All went well on my initiation to carrier flying but that was not the case with all flights during this working-up period. I was in the second of two Avengers waiting to take off when my pilot said, "He's gone in," obviously referring to the first one. Looking out on the port side, I caught a glimpse of the aircraft floating by with the pilot scrambling out. As my pilot had been instructed to cut his engine, I joined others on the flight deck, by which time the aircraft had disappeared but astern could be seen the head of the pilot in the sea. Some seconds later, another head appeared and we waited for the third; by this time the ship had left them well astern and they appeared as small dots on the surface. Our anxiety grew as there was no sign of the third member of the crew, but just as we were fearing the worst, a third black dot suddenly appeared. The crew were safely rescued by the attendant escort vessel and we later heard of their experience. The aircraft had failed to reach flying speed when leaving the deck and had slipped to port, just avoiding being hit by the ship. Hitting the sea, it remained afloat long enough to allow the pilot to get out, but for the observer and TAG, both on the bench seat in the lower cabin, escape was not so easily accomplished. The cabin door, on the starboard side, had to be jettisoned before escape was possible and this while the cabin filled with water. In the event, the observer, who was nearest the door, managed to free himself but the TAG, Fred Alldred, seems to have been knocked unconscious and remembered little of his escape. The arrangement whereby the observer and TAG sat in the cabin for take-off and landing was later changed, the observer sat in the centre section cockpit and the TAG in the turret. There had, of course, been other mishaps during the flying at Quonset, but this was the first time that crew members' lives had been seriously threatened and, for those of us watching events from the safety of the ship, it was a timely reminder of the dangers of carrier flying.

After a day in port, *Chaser* sailed for New York on 20th June arriving there the next day. The ship tied up at Staten Island and squadron personnel had two more opportunities for shore leave in New York. I took both, and note that the times of my return to the ship were 0330 and 0430, so sleep must have been severely curtailed! We put to sea on 23rd June and joined Convoy HX245, west of Halifax, bound for the UK; the squadron was to undertake its first operational duties by providing air cover for the convoy.

Convoy HX245 was the largest to attempt the Atlantic crossing at that time, comprising ninety-one ships, varying in type, size and nationality, arranged in thirteen columns of seven with escort vessels patrolling the perimeter. *Chaser* was positioned in the middle of the convoy which, at the time, gave us a certain sense of security against U-boat attack; a totally wrong assumption, as the U-boat tactics were to penetrate the convoy and select the most important ships for attack.

Air cover for the convoy was to be shared by 845 Avengers on *Chaser* and the 836 Swordfish on *Empire MacAlpine*. The latter was the first Merchant Aircraft Carrier, returning from her maiden voyage, and was loaded with 10,000 tons of grain which made her less lively in the Atlantic swell than the *Chaser*. The Swordfish were able to operate in conditions which would have been hazardous for the Avengers. However, a few days out, the MAC-ship, while manoeuvring to allow her aircraft to land, collided with merchantman *Empire Ibex* and for the rest of the passage was unable to operate aircraft except in emergency. So the *Chaser* had to provide all air cover demands which, in effect, meant two aircraft on patrol from dawn to dusk. One Avenger would patrol ten miles ahead of the convoy while the other was astern; flights being between two and three hours in duration. My crew had just finished one such patrol and were the first in the landing circuit, which proved providential that day. For landing on, the TAG now sat in the turret facing aft so could not see when touchdown was imminent. However, as the aircraft approached the stern of the carrier, he could judge by the whiteness of the ship's wake, the distance from the round-down and, by looking over his right shoulder, he would catch a glimpse of the batsman before the aircraft hit the deck. In this way, he was able to brace himself for the impact when seven tons of Avenger, travelling at 75 knots, was jerked to a stop by the arrester hook engaging one of the wires across the flight deck. On this occasion, I looked round as usual, saw the batsman, and braced myself for the violent deceleration when the hook caught the wire. But none came; instead, we floated along the deck above the wires and I braced myself even harder, waiting for the crash into the barrier, but again nothing happened. We continued to float serenely on and, as we passed the island, I wondered what those on the bridge thought of our antics. Then my reverie ended with a bang as we hit the deck near the forward lift and my thoughts turned involuntarily to the Avenger which had gone over the side in the previous week. Up to the time of impact, my pilot had made no attempt to abort the landing and go round again, so the engine was still throttled back; however, the violence of the impact and, no doubt, the sight of the fast-disappearing deck space ahead stimulated him into action. The throttle was opened wide and the aircraft bounded forward along the remaining 100 feet of deck, and over the end we went, dropping down, but still maintaining flying speed. As we skimmed the wave tops, I found myself trying to ease the weight off my seat as if it would, in some fashion, stop us sinking into the sea. After a time, we gained height and on our second approach landed safely, which was just as well as the second Avenger had now landed and was parked forward of the crash barrier. If these had been the circumstances of our first landing, the barrier could not have been lowered and a crash would have been inevitable. Our flight over the deck was of the order of five seconds, but at the time it seemed unending.

The flying of anti-submarine patrols for 16 hours each day meant that the squadron ground crews were put under great pressure to ensure maximum serviceability of aircraft. Jim Mackenzie, the senior radio mechanic, gives his recollections of the trip.

'Apart from the routine maintenance, much of our time was spent in ranging and striking down aircraft. With someone on the brakes, four more on the wheel-chocks, and others helping to push or pull the seven ton monsters, we manipulated them into position around the hangar. Then there was the loading and unloading of the four 325lb depth charges carried by each Avenger while on patrol. Our armourers had devised a quick method for unloading them using a pile of hammock mattresses placed under the bomb-bay, one side at a time, and then operating the release button in the cockpit. The inevitable happened; with the mattresses under the port side the armourer released a depth charge on the starboard side, which hit the deck with an almighty clang and rolled away under parked aircraft pursued by a few brave souls with the rest of us transfixed waiting for the bang.

'Day after day the routine continued, with no sightings of the enemy or alarms of any kind; against the odds, it seemed that we were living a charmed life. There was one anxious period when *Chaser* had to stop engines for about half an hour to effect repairs. Sitting stationary in mid-Atlantic with the convoy slowly disappearing over the horizon is an unnerving experience even with a couple of frigates doing sweeps around us. Finally, we were in sight of land and the ship docked at Greenock on 6th July.'

At the time, we had counted ourselves as lucky to have escaped the attentions of the U-boats and it was many years before we learned that, following the disastrous losses in May, of 41 U-boats, Admiral Dönitz had withdrawn his wolf-packs from the North Atlantic. Nevertheless, for those of us on the convoy the fear of attack was real enough.

The squadron stayed on the *Chaser* for a couple of days and was then sent on two weeks leave and instructed to return to RNAS Hatston in the Orkneys. Together with a fellow TAG, I made my way to Glasgow station for our journey south. Having some time to wait before the departure of our train, my companion left to do some local shopping while I kept an eye on our luggage in the station concourse. I wandered around, never straying too far away while keeping a good watch, as I thought, on our bags. After a visit to a nearby bookstall, I glanced down and realised that the two small navy cases of mine were no longer there. I raced around looking everywhere but in the crowds it was a lost cause. When my companion had returned, I reported the theft to the police and we caught the next train home. The cases stolen were the ones containing all the presents which I had purchased in America including items in short supply in the UK such as ladies stockings and a bunch of bananas. The latter had been bought in Norfolk, green and unripe, but, after two weeks, were looking decidedly over-ripe but nevertheless recognisable as bananas which were virtually unobtainable in the UK. I was somewhat annoyed, mainly with myself for being outwitted by a thief, and reconciled myself to not seeing the articles again. A week or so later, I received notice from the local police that they had something belonging to me so I went along to collect it. I was shown one of the cases with my name stamped on it; the side had been cut out and was empty except for a large photograph. It was one of myself with my pilot taken on a trip to Hamilton Standard Propellers while in the States and reproduced in this book. On reflection, it was the one item in the cases which I would have regretted losing.

* * * *

846 Squadron moved from USNAS Quonset to Brunswick, Maine, for the last month of their training then travelled to Norfolk, Virginia, where it embarked on *Ravager*, a newly-commissioned escort carrier, on 2nd July. One of the squadron aircraft was delayed by engine trouble and was to join the ship on the following day; John Minards was the TAG of that crew.

'The ship was out in Chesapeake Bay waiting for our arrival and as we approached I felt a little apprehensive, as it was our first carrier landing as a crew. The observer and I were seated on the bench seat in the rear cabin in accordance with prevailing regulations. The aircraft approached the stern of the ship and then, as the hook caught the arrester wire, there was a tremendous jerk and we were down. I had started to breathe a sigh of relief, when I realised that the aircraft had developed a distinct tilt to port and was slipping inexorably towards the side of the ship; the reason being the collapse of the port undercarriage leg. Suddenly, we dropped like a stone and hit the water with our port wing, leaving the rear cabin door above water long enough for the observer to jettison it and then, using my face as a stepping stone, he was out, followed very quickly by me. By this time, the ship had left us far behind, but the stand-by vessel, a US Coast Guard cutter, was soon alongside and hauled us out. They even apologised for being "a dry ship" but, even so, we were grateful for their prompt attention.'

In the afternoon, John's aircraft ditched again, this time on take-off, the engine losing power owing to a faulty throttle-damper. Then, on the next morning, when the squadron was scheduled for boosted takeoffs, his aircraft once again crashed into the sea. On this occasion, the ditching was caused by the catapult sling being incorrectly attached to the Avenger. John and his crew were fortunate to escape alive and uninjured from their ditchings as events, a few days later, showed. While continuing to work up, in Chesapeake Bay, the squadron lost its first crew when an Avenger stalled on take-off and crashed into the sea. Leading Airman D. Ritchie was the TAG of the crew which was killed; the funeral took place at Evergreen Memorial Park, Portsmouth, Virginia, on 10th July.

The *Ravager* then sailed for New York where it joined a convoy to provide air cover for its passage to the UK. On 27th July, the squadron flew off to RNAS Macrihanish, and, on the next day, from there to RNAS Hatston.

* * * *

848 Squadron formed up at USNAS Quonset on 1st June, 1943, staying there for six weeks before moving to USNAS Brunswick and then USNAS Squantum to complete their training. Embarking on the escort carrier *Trumpeter* at the beginning of September, the squadron, after working up with the ship, provided anti-submarine patrols for the voyage to the UK.

* * * *

849 Squadron formed-up at USNAS Quonset Point on 1st August, 1943, the last Avenger squadron to do so there. A proportion of the personnel was sent over from the UK but a number were transferred from the resident Training Unit whose job had now finished. The squadron left Quonset after a few weeks and completed their training at USNAS Squantum, Massachusetts. In training, one crew was lost when its aircraft dived into the sea during a dummy torpedo attack, a few miles off Cape Cod; the TAG was Leading Airman W.E.J. Thomson. On 1st November, the squadron moved to Norfolk, Virginia, where it boarded *Khedive*, a newly-commissioned escort carrier, for passage to the UK.

* * * *

On paper, 850 Squadron was formed at USNAS Quonset Point on 1st January, 1943, to be equipped with Curtiss Seamews but, in fact, the plan did not materialise and the theoretical squadron was disbanded on 30th of the same month. Therefore, the squadron of Avengers which was formed at Squantum on 1st September, 1943, was, on paper at least, reforming. During their training there, one crew was lost on a night flying exercise when their aircraft was seen to crash into the sea; the TAG was Leading Airman T.C. Williams.

Having finished their training at Squantum, 850 moved to the Seal Island RCAF Station, Vancouver, where it spent two months waiting to join *Empress* which was in dock at Vancouver. In January, deck landing training began with *Empress*, and working-up with the ship continued until the middle of February, when it set sail for the long journey home. The squadron carried out U-Boat patrols during the passage and flew into RNAS Lee-on-Solent on 10th April.

* * * *

Having finished their Avenger training at Squantum, 851 Squadron was sent to the US naval base at Alameda, near San Francisco, to join *Shah*, a newly commissioned escort carrier. The aircraft were flown the 3,500 miles without mishap, having eight stops during the five days trip. The rest of the squadron travelled by train, also taking five days to reach their destination. After a week or so at Alameda, the *Shah* arrived from Vancouver and the squadron embarked. Also taken aboard were 50 or so aircraft as freight thus making any flying impossible.

Of the squadron TAGs, eight of them were from 45A Course trained in Canada and had been drafted direct to 851 after completing their training. Larry Larwood was one of them and recalls,

'All previous squadrons had returned to the UK and we, not unnaturally, expected to do likewise. However, in the second half of January, 1944, the *Shah* chugged out into San Francisco Bay, under the Golden Gate Bridge, and out into the Pacific bound for India via Australia, without escort. It was over two months later before we reached Cochin in Southern India where all aircraft were put ashore, only to have our own aircraft brought back on board. Finally, we put to sea and started flying.'

* * * *

852 Squadron had completed training at Squantum by the end of January, 1944, and was then faced with joining its carrier on the west coast. The aircraft were flown across, taking some ground crew as passengers to service them on the 3,500 mile journey. At Lynchburg, Virginia, one of the stops on the way to San Francisco, one Avenger did a ground loop and was so badly damaged that it had to be abandoned and a replacement aircraft obtained to finish the journey. The TAG, Leading Airman A.G. Stocker and two Air Mechanics were the passengers but amazingly neither they nor the pilot were injured.

The remaining personnel travelled by train and, with the whole squadron together again, it went aboard *Nabob*, a new escort carrier, on 11th February. Once again, the working-up process brought together a new ship and a new squadron both needing to learn from each other to achieve operational competence in their respective roles.

Soon the ship set sail down the coast to San Diego, through the Panama Canal then up the east coast, putting in at Norfolk, Virginia, for minor repairs; a lot of flying was done and anti-submarine patrols maintained. Then it was on to New York where the ship was loaded with Mustang fighters for transhipment, making it a non-flying voyage to the UK. The squadron flew ashore to RNAS Macrihanish on 6th April.

* * * *

853 Squadron formed up at Squantum on 1st December, 1943, and started flying their brand new Avengers on the 6th. On the next day, Blue Flight were making a practice torpedo attack on a small island, off the coast, when one of the three aircraft dived into the sea with the loss of the crew, including the TAG, Leading Airman D.E. Afford. It was a most tragic beginning for a new squadron.

Having completed their training at Squantum, 853 Squadron were to join *Arbiter*, an escort carrier, in Vancouver, which meant crossing from the east to the west coast. In 1944, the established route for single-engined aircraft was to fly south to the Mexican border and then north up the west coast. The journey by air was estimated to take 4 days, which was the same time as for the ground crews going by train but, in the event, the flight, owing to accidents and engine troubles, took 10 days. They stayed at the RCAF base south of Vancouver for three weeks, during which time deck-landing practice and formation flying were carried out.

On 5th April, 1944, the squadron flew aboard *Arbiter* and within a few days had set sail for New York via the Panama Canal. The voyage proved to be a lengthy one as the ship broke down on two occasions, having to be towed into a nearby port for repairs. Some flying was undertaken but not without having one aircraft lost over the side and two more damaged in landing crashes. Finally, on 31st May, the ship docked in Brooklyn, over three months since they had flown over New York on their way to Vancouver. After another eight days, during which the flight deck was loaded with Corsair fighters for transhipment, *Arbiter* joined a UK convoy arriving at Glasgow on 20th June. There the Avengers were unloaded, taken to the nearby Renfrew airfield and flown to the RNAS at Macrihanish.

* * * *

After completing their training at Squantum, 854 Squadron left for Norfolk, Virginia, on 9th April and boarded *Indomitable*, which had been out of action since 11th July, 1943, after being torpedoed off Sicily. The next day, the aircraft were hoisted aboard from the dockside but due to the size and weight of the Avenger, there were handling difficulties on the lifts and in the hangar. Then followed a short period of working up with the ship in Chesapeake Bay and on 12th April the first Avenger flew from *Indomitable*. The ship sailed for the UK on the 20th and flew ashore to RNAS Macrihanish on 2nd May.

* * * *

855 Squadron formed-up at Squantum on 1st February, 1944, and was disbanded just over eight months later, the shortest existence of any of the 15 Avenger squadrons. After completion of the training programme, at the end of April, 855 went to Norfolk, Virginia, where it embarked on the newly commissioned escort carrier *Queen* for passage to the UK. By the end of May, the squadron was at the RAF base at Hawkinge forming, with 854 Squadron, No.157 (GR) Wing under the control of Coastal Command. There was to be little working-up before commencing operations in the Channel.

* * * *

856 Squadron formed at Squantum on 1st March, 1944, and a number of the TAG complement were from No.49A Course, having just finished their training at the No.2 TAG School at Yarmouth, Canada. One of these, Leading Airman H. Seddon, was killed when his aircraft failed to return from a night bombing exercise off Cape Cod on March 14. Having finished their training, 856 flew down to Norfolk, Virginia, on 1st June to join a newly commissioned escort carrier, *Smiter*, for passage to the UK. The ship put in to New York where TAG, Alf

Austin, on a trip ashore, recalls standing in Times Square on D-Day watching the news headlines flash up on the neon signs, "US and Allied Troops Invade Europe". Shortly after, the *Smiter* sailed for the UK in a convoy of 25 ships with 5 USN escort vessels. The *Smiter* docked at Liverpool on June 20 and the next day, the aircraft were unloaded by crane and towed to the airfield at nearby Speke from where they were flown to RNAS Macrihanish the following day.

* * * *

At the end of February, 1944, 857 personnel sailed for the USA and at Squantum, on 1st April, the squadron was officially formed. It was to be the last Avenger squadron to form-up in the USA and after training 857 travelled to Norfolk, Virginia, where it embarked on escort carrier *Rajah* for passage to the UK, going ashore at RNAS Belfast where its complement was increased to 21 aircraft. From there, the squadron moved to RNAS Macrihanish for three weeks of anti-submarine training before re-embarking on *Rajah*. At Macrihanish, Bill Pirie, who was senior TAG, was promoted to Chief Petty Officer Airman in accordance with current regulations; what was rather unusual was to be told by the Station Commander that, in his view, Bill's length of service did not justify him being a CPO so that it was with reluctance that he confirmed the promotion. Not exactly a vote of confidence! In September, *Rajah* sailed for Ceylon where 857 was to join the *Indomitable*.

* * * *

820, equipped with Barracudas, served on *Indefatigable* during the attacks on the *Tirpitz* in August, 1944; disembarking to RNAS Macrihanish in September and then moving to Lee-on-Solent where it re-equipped with Avengers. At the same time, it merged with 826 Squadron and the complement of aircraft was increased to 21. One of the TAGs drafted to the squadron was Roy Gibbs who, with his crew, were sent from their OTU squadron to Macrihanish only to find that 820 had moved to Lee. There, he was dismayed to find himself flying with another crew and his dismay increased when his trip in an Avenger finished by crashing into a field of cabbages behind the airfield. However, on his release from sick-bay, he was delighted to discover that he was re-united with his old crew, with whom he served for the rest of the war. He found that training flights in the south coast area, while the war in France was still raging, had their dangers; trigger-happy gunners on the ships in the Solent would sometimes open up despite the D-Day black and white stripes painted on their Avengers. However, in a few short weeks, they were ordered to make ready to join *Indefatigable*, the same fleet carrier upon which the squadron had served previously.

* * * *

828 Squadron, equipped with Barracudas, had served aboard *Implacable*, a fleet carrier newly commissioned in August, 1944, which had been involved in a series of shipping strikes off Norway during the latter half of 1944. The strength of the squadron was increased to 21 aircraft by the absorption of 841, also a Barracuda squadron. At the beginning of February, 1945, 828 moved to RNAS Fearn, where it was re-equipped with Avengers described by one of the TAGs as "a motley collection, previously used for drogue-towing, etcetera". For the next six weeks, 828 completed their familiarisation training and, on 9th March, embarked on *Implacable* en route for Ceylon. With 828, there were now four squadrons aboard making a total complement of around 80 aircraft, twice the number for which the ship was designed, creating problems with their storage, maintenance and operation. Perhaps of more significance was the serious overcrowding of living quarters with the extra squadron personnel. The problem was to become even more acute in the Pacific when USN liaison staff came on board.

HOME WATERS

Towards the end of July, 845 Squadron personnel returned from leave to RNAS Hatston, near Kirkwall in the Orkneys, where they were to remain until the end of the year. Flying began immediately and continued ceaselessly throughout the period despite the adverse weather conditions affecting the region during late autumn. For example, my log for October shows 40 flights and 39 for November. The programme covered every type of exercise, torpedo, bombing, air-firing, fighter evasion, navigation, and radar being the main ones.

The squadron still continued with simulated torpedo attacks and for these the Home Fleet ships were often the targets; on August 14th, for example, the squadron made a combined attack, with a Barracuda squadron, on the Home Fleet which had put to sea for the occasion with Their Majesties, The King and Queen, aboard the *Duke of York,* which was accompanied by *Anson, Renown,* and destroyer escorts. In addition to these simulated attacks, where no missiles were dropped, exercises with dummy torpedoes were carried out, allowing the pilots to get accustomed to handling the aircraft with the additional weight of the torpedo and to practise its release. Finally, attacks were made with live torpedoes, but without the warheads. For the TAG, these exercises involved only a minimum of radio communication so he was free to sit back and enjoy them, the slow climb to 10,000 feet, flying in formation, the location of the target ship, looking like a child's toy boat in a pond, the dive to sea-level, the run-in for release of the torpedo and finally the evasive manoeuvres while leaving the target area. If sat in the lower cabin during the dive, he was made more conscious of descent by the rapidly unwinding altimeter, the sight of the sea rushing ever closer, and the buffeting from the wind in the open bomb-bay. In the turret, the TAG was subject to an entirely different sensation, one of disorientation arising from his position facing aft which meant that it was like falling headfirst but backwards. In both cases he was made aware of the speed of the dive by the severity of the pressure on his eardrums. Pulling out of the dive was the climax of the trip and any nervous tension soon ebbed away. One thought little of the pilot having to struggle to control the seven ton monster as it raced earthwards at 300 knots; perhaps it was a measure of the confidence in his ability to fly the Avenger but more likely it was sheer ignorance of the pilot's task!

At the time, it seemed that the squadron had been chosen for extensive torpedo training with a particular object in view and this idea was supported when, on several occasions, the squadron was alerted to stand-by for action and aircraft were armed with torpedoes. The reason for these alerts was never forthcoming but conjecture would indicate that they were caused by the threat of German heavy warships breaking out into the North Sea. It was unfortunate that on September 27, when an attempted torpedo strike on a German warship was launched from Hatston, 845 was on leave until the 28th! There must have been a change of policy with regard to using the Avenger as a torpedo bomber because the end of November saw the entry "ALT" in my log for the last time. From then on, glide bombing was the primary function of the squadron.

Air-firing exercises continued at intervals but results were far from satisfactory; my own figures for hits recorded on the target drogue were still of the order of a few percent with the occasional zero. The drogue was, of course, much smaller than a fighter aircraft and so a greater number of hits would be expected on the latter, whilst the hitting power of the 0.5-in Browning was tremendous and so fewer hits would be required to cause serious damage. However, a fighter aircraft would not be such an easy target to hit as a drogue and with evasive manoeuvres being taken the chance of hits would be slim. Add to this, the high incident of stoppages and failures with the turret gun and the picture gets even worse. Perhaps, it was the effect of our Chief TAG giving us a lecture on the need for us to give greater attention to our guns' maintenance which induced me to follow his advice. Normally, all maintenance was done by the squadron armourers and TAGs were only too pleased to leave it that way, myself included. On this occasion, I decided to harmonise the turret gun to see if it would improve my shooting accuracy. This entailed lining up the barrel of the gun on a target at a defined range, say, 400 yards, and then lining up the sight on the same target; simple really, or so I thought. In fact, trying to locate the white target board while crouching on the turret seat to peer into a periscope placed in the barrel was a most difficult task mainly because of the physical restrictions occasioned by the turret. After much effort and not a little cursing, for my stupidity in attempting the job in the first place, I managed to align the barrel and all that was left to do was line up the reflector sight and lock it into position. That done, I closed the top plate and released the bolt which I had cocked to enable me to look through the barrel. Feeling rather pleased with myself, I returned to the squadron offices and then I remembered that I must return the periscope which I had borrowed from the armourers. Then it hit me, the realisation that I had not removed the periscope before releasing the bolt on the gun. I ran back to the aircraft, scrambled into the turret, drew back the bolt and looked inside to see the mangled remains of the periscope protruding from the chamber of the barrel. I will not relate the consequences of my actions other than to say that I never undertook the harmonisation of my gun again!

From later discussions with armourers and TAGs, I believe that the gun was highly accurate on a firm base, but the turret did not provide that for such a powerful gun hence the poor results. However, for firing at a stationary target, when strafing for example, it was superb as it could be used like a hose-pipe to spray the target. The problem of operating faults with the gun were also due, to some degree, to the turret which was so cramped, especially for anyone over 5 feet 5 inches, that the clearance of single stoppages was quite awkward. The operation of the turret itself also caused problems as there had to be electrical cutouts to prevent the gun from firing when it was being traversed past parts of the aircraft and every electrical contact was a potential source of breakdown. It was not impossible for the TAG to be trapped upside down in the turret when operating the high-speed button, a device for increasing the speed of movement of the turret, in which case release was only possible with outside assistance. In effect, it was inadvisable to use the device as the consequences could be, at least, embarrassing or, at worst, fatal.

It was the former case for TAG, Stewart Crawford, while serving with 856 Squadron on *Premier*. On the second occasion when he was stuck in the turret, the weather was less than favourable for deck landings and so permission was requested to fly to the nearest land base, which was RNAS Hatston some 200 miles away. After a long and, for Stewart, uncomfortable flight, they came in to Hatston where a crowd of curious onlookers had gathered to see them land. He was soon released from the turret and so, after refreshments at the NAAFI, they took off to return to *Premier*. He never used the high-speed button again!

Fighter evasion exercises were introduced for the first time and were of two distinct types. The first was designed for a single Avenger being attacked by a fighter from astern and involved corkscrewing manoeuvres to prevent the fighter aligning his guns upon the Avenger when in firing range, say, 400 to 600 yards. As the fighter commenced his approach, the observer would warn the pilot to stand by for a turn to port or starboard; if the approach was from the port quarter, the warning would be to dive to port and vice versa. When the observer judged the fighter to be in range, he would tell the pilot to dive port or starboard as the case might be. In this way, the fighter would be forced to tighten his approach curve and, if the ploy was successful, be unable to follow the Avenger and thus would have to break off the attack. During this manoeuvre, the TAG would be attempting to operate the turret gun fitted with cine-camera to record his "firing" performance for analysis later. For the TAG, a diving turn to port was the worst, for then he suddenly found himself looking down at the ground, some 5,000 feet below, with just a flimsy sheet of Perspex between him and the earth. At the same time, he was subject to alternate forces of G and Negative G while attempting to train the turret on the attacking fighter. It was stomach-churning work but one felt that it might some day save your skin and was therefore worth doing.

In the second type of exercise, the squadron flew in formation and were subject to simulated attacks by fighters while the TAGs operated their turret guns equipped with cine-cameras. The resulting films were analysed to show how effective the combined turret fire would have been against enemy fighters and to examine the possibility of improving the level of effectiveness. It was on one of these exercises that the squadron lost its first crew.

On 9th October, nine Avengers took off and, having formed up, headed west across Scapa knowing that they were to be "attacked" by a Seafire from Skeabrae, a satellite of Hatston, at any time. John Munro, one of the TAGs, witnessed the tragedy at close quarters.

'I was in the leading plane of a sub-flight of three with the other two no more than 40 feet away on either side. I spotted the Seafire approaching and swung the turret round to meet the attack. I was watching through my gun-sight as it grew bigger and bigger and swung the turret round to keep it in sight as it banked to starboard. The Seafire hit the wing of the Avenger on my starboard side slicing off part of the end. For a brief instant I saw the TAG, PO Airman Gavin Rough, looking towards me from his turret before the plane began its fatal plunge into the sea some thousand feet below. I shall never forget the look of surprise and then horror on his face. Watching the plane, for the ten seconds or so, before it hit the sea was a sickening experience.'

* * * *

Gavin Rough was well liked on the squadron, a sportsman of some merit and newly-married. He had, in 1942, been shot down during the invasion of Madagascar while serving with 827 Squadron on *Indomitable*. After ditching, he and his crew were stranded on an uninhabited island for over a month before being rescued on the point of starvation. It was tragic that he should have survived for such an end. A few days earlier, he had won a marathon race at Hatston and the winner's trophy was named in his memory.

* * * *

Bombing exercises were quite numerous and were of two main types, glide-bombing and anti-submarine bombing. The former were carried out on static targets, diving from about 5,000 feet and releasing the practice bombs at around 1,500 feet. A/S bombing exercises were performed on static and towed targets with the release height down to 100 feet; on the basis that in real attacks depth charges would be used and these, like the practice bomb, would be no danger to the low flying aircraft. A special bombing technique introduced at this time was the Bogue Method, which entailed making a short, steep dive onto the target after a shallow glide approach; presumably a way of getting dive bombing accuracy without building up speed to over 300 knots as would be the case in a long steep approach.

Some of the bombing exercises were carried out at night and, on two occasions, owing to an unexpected change in the weather, we found ourselves enveloped in low cloud and lost our bearings. On both occasions, we had to ask for the assistance of the D/F stations to give us the bearings to lead us back to base. In such hilly terrain, the course back would sometimes be quite intricate as when you approached the base you had to descend possibly to a few hundred feet before seeing the runway so any variation from the course given could be fatal. The worst occasion was after bombing Stack Skerry, an island to the west of Hatston, when the flight lasted for almost three hours, two of which were spent trying to locate the base. We were the last aircraft to land and even then it was at the RAF station at Skeabrae not Hatston which had been forced to close because of impossible landing conditions. As the TAG, the responsibility for maintaining contact with the D/F station kept you busy and so helped to keep your mind off the consequences of not finding the drome.

On 3rd December, the CO of the squadron, L/Cdr W.H. Crawford, RN, left Hatston having been replaced by L/Cdr (A) J.F. Arnold. He was flown to Inverness airport by my pilot and I recall wondering what he thought of being a back-seat passenger sharing the cabin with the TAG. It also confirmed my belief in my pilot's flying ability for, as the ex-CO, he would certainly be aware of the pilots who were the safest to fly with, even on a cross-country trip.

The squadron completed its flying programme at Hatston on

Christmas Eve, 1943, a period of four months, allowing for home leave, which was similar to that spent on the training programme at Quonset. However, at Hatston, I recorded 132 flights, amounting to 151 hours of flying time, double the number at Quonset, a fact which indicates the intensity of the flying programme. Apart from the loss of a crew in October, the squadron had not experienced any other serious accidents but John Munro had a near escape when he went for a short test flight in a new Avenger.

'It was 1610 on 23rd, when Gus Halliday, the pilot, and I took off for a short trip to check the aircraft. As we passed over St. Magnus Cathedral, in nearby Kirkwall, at about 800 feet, I looked down at the spire below and at that moment, the aircraft started to shake violently and I saw red sparks and what appeared to be molten metal passing the cabin window on the starboard side. Gus came on the intercom and said something about a parachute which, as it was only for a short flight, I had not bothered to bring and as I was telling him of my plight the intercom went dead. Thinking that we should have to ditch, I found myself worrying about the two weeks' pay in my pocket, about £12, which, being Friday, I had only received that day. At least, that took my mind off the uncomfortable manoeuvres which were going on as the pilot struggled to land the plane safely which he did with consummate skill. Even from our low height, he had managed to bring the Avenger down on the rough grass within the airfield perimeter; the only damage, apart from the engine, of course, was the removal of part of the port wing. We had been airborne for just five minutes. My failure to take a parachute was a serious offence as it could have endangered other persons lives but nothing was said and in a few days the squadron had left Hatston.'

The squadron left Hatston at 0800 on Monday, 3rd January, bound for RNAS Macrihanish, a remote spot on the south-west coast of the Kintyre Peninsula, and arrived there at 1730 the following day. It was a nightmare journey, starting with the sea trip across the Pentland Firth then at its stormiest. At Thurso, we waited for the 0800 train to Perth, which had neither heating nor lighting thus making the ten hour journey an exceedingly uncomfortable affair. However, considerably heartened by a good breakfast, we caught the 7am train to Glasgow arriving 9.30am. The mode of transport was then changed to buses upon which we toiled our way along winding roads amidst marvellous scenery which we were in no mood to appreciate. The journey seemed unending and several stops were made for refreshments and to stretch weary limbs. We finally arrived at 1730 having been in transit for 33½ hours in freezing conditions.

The squadron stayed at Macrihanish just for the month of January, which I recall as a cold, wet and stormy period so much so that flying programmes were continually having to be postponed. Nevertheless, they were completed by the simple expedient of flying extra trips on those days when conditions were at all possible; on a number of dates, my log shows flying in the morning, afternoon and night. Most were bombing exercises, usually 4 sticks of two bombs on fixed or towed targets, but the night exercises involved locating submarines on the surface by radar and illuminating them by flares for feint attacks. Between these days of high activity, were periods of utter boredom, with the stormy weather conditions limiting the scope for utilising any free time which might be granted. Apart from any entertainment which the camp might offer, the only outside alternative was Campbeltown, some four miles away, which boasted a WVS canteen and a cinema and little else which I can recall. However, I did achieve one success while at Macrihanish; I took and passed the examinations for the confirmation of my rank as Leading Airman, which meant, in practice that you were then entitled to request promotion to Acting Petty Officer - a worthwhile move both as regards pay and status.

Macrihanish was an important naval air station used by many front-line squadrons while disembarked from their carriers which used the Firth of Clyde and Irish Sea for their working-up operations. Accordingly, there were a number of bombing ranges in the area which catered for the differing requirements of the various squadrons.

Although the basic feature of a bombing range was the provision of a target, of equal importance was the recording of the results of the bombing exercises so that performances could be monitored and, where necessary, action taken to raise standards to acceptable levels. In the recording process, Wrens, classified as Bomb Range Markers, were responsible for performing this task.

* * * *

There were four ranges located on the Kintyre peninsula; at Ballure and Bellochantuy on the west coast and at Crossaig and Skipness on the east. At each range, the target was positioned about a mile off shore and was of triangular construction in the centre of which was a sighting pole for the use of the bomb markers and an aiming roundel for the bombing aircraft. On shore, were two observation posts, known as quadrant huts, two-storey buildings of brick construction with windows facing the target. The huts were spaced some distance apart so that their sighting lines to the target formed a right angle. When a bombing exercise was in process, two simultaneous observations were made from each hut in respect of each attack made, one recorded the height of the bomb release and the other the bearing from the hut of the bomb's impact. In the latter case, when the two bearings were plotted, their point of intersection marked the point where the bomb landed. In making these observations, the markers used glass screens, appropriately graduated, with sighting devices for observing the bomb release from the ground floor position and the bomb impact from the upper floor. The graduations on the screens gave the appropriate information either the height of release or the bearing of the bomb impact; this information was passed by one quadrant hut to the other which, equipped with telephone, transmitted the information to the plotting office at Macrihanish. Prior to the exercise, the staff at the ranges would be given the full details of the aircraft which would be using the range, including the number and sequence of the aircraft so that each could be identified with the observations made. Communication with the aircraft, where necessary, was by means of the Aldis lamp, using morse. For night exercises, the same procedures were operated by the light of the flares dropped by the aircraft before their bombing runs. The small parachutes attached to the flares were eagerly sought by the Wrens, as the white nylon from which they were made could be used for making items of underwear. However, they were not alone in realising the usefulness of the parachutes, local inhabitants would also join in the search, so off-duty Wrens might even start looking while the bombing exercise was still in progress.

The Wrens engaged on the ranges were all quartered at Skipness, a small village overlooking the Kilbrannan Sound and Isle of Arran. The group comprised 40 or so markers, 2 cooks, 2 MT drivers and POs, with a Second Officer in charge. Their quarters, wooden huts in the grounds of Skipness House, were fairly primitive, with no electricity supply, lighting being provided by Tilley lamps. When not on duty on the ranges, the Wrens undertook all the other duties relating to the running of the quarters and galley. Transport was provided by their own two 15 cwt trucks, which took the teams of markers to the various ranges depending upon the bombing programme for the day; Bellochantuy range, at 25 miles distance, was the farthest away. The self-sufficiency of the group, away from the direct control of their base at Macrihanish, and the specialist nature of their duties, which brought them in contact with the more adventurous elements of the Service, tended to foster a justifiable pride in their unit. The nature of their duties meant that they were witnessing each day, at close quarters, the practising of the ultimate action against the enemy, its elimination. Inevitably, they also saw the consequences when things went wrong and aircraft crashed while performing their practice runs. On one such occasion, at Crossaig, they were able to rescue the pilot of a crashed aircraft, who was taken by the MT driver, Beth Booth, to the RN hospital at Southend, some thirty miles away, for which action she was awarded the BEM. It is scarcely surprising that they were popular with the squadrons training there and this fact was confirmed in writing by 831 whose members composed the Ode to Skipness Rangers after a party at the Skipness Quarters. However, with the finish of the war in Europe, the requirement for the bombing ranges declined, but the need for similar facilities in the Far East increased. Valerie Bain (née Chenery) was drafted from Skipness to RNAS Katukurunda, Ceylon, where she worked, as a Range Marker, on the ranges at Payagala and Maggone, which were used, among others, by the Avenger squadrons.

* * * *

At the end of January, 845 were on the move again, this time just an hour's flight across the North Channel to RNAS Maydown in Northern Ireland. As the living quarters, at the main camp, were some distance from the airfield, we were equipped with bicycles to make our own way; quite an innovation which gave us TAGs some simple pleasure as we rode in formation of threes down the taxi-ways. The object of the visit to Maydown was for the aircrew to attend an anti U-boat course; a combination of classroom lectures and practical exercises. There was an outline of the U-boat war, detailing the parts played by the Royal Navy and Coastal Command, finishing with the current developments in tactics by both sides. The main emphasis was on the latest move by the Germans to increase the anti-aircraft armament on U-boats and, when attacked, to stay on the surface and use its greater fire power to deter the attacker. The result could then be stalemate, either the aircraft risked being shot down or kept its distance until forced to abandon the attack because of lack of fuel. The solution to the problem was for the aircraft to be able to call up assistance in the form of either fighter aircraft or surface ships and to this end practical exercises were devised. Homing exercises were carried out with corvettes, based at nearby Londonderry, wherein individual aircraft would make radio contact, on a prescribed wavelength, and home the corvette to their position some 30 miles or so distant. Alternatively, Wildcat aircraft would be vectored to the aircraft and then a combined attack made on a target submarine. The aim was a simultaneous attack by Avenger and Wildcat, the latter attacking from stem to stern so as to keep the submarine's gunners quiet while the depth charges were dropped athwart by the Avenger. It called for split-second timing if the charges were to be dropped before the gunners had time to recover from the

Wildcat's strafing and even the simulated attacks could raise the heart-beat a trifle. Apart from the latter, the flying was rather mundane and not much of it, consequently, there was plenty of free time with Londonderry and Belfast to visit.

While attending one of the classroom lectures, I was informed that I was supposed to be at Captain's requestmen which were then being presented. I hurried off but was not there when my name was called, however, I was seen later and promoted to Acting Petty Officer Airman. I was euphoric and rushed back to the camp to sew a PO's badge on my tunic and to change my messing quarters; the suddenness of the promotion added to the excitement of the occasion. However, the pleasure of being one of the "no-badge POs" soon began to fade as their numbers proliferated, especially in the TAG and Radio & Radar Branches where, under new regulations, the rank could be achieved in two years. In the Navy proper, where POs would normally have served in excess of three years and would therefore have at least one Good Conduct Badge, the term was used in derision rather than as a compliment. The effect was to increase the number of POs on a squadron of 12 Avengers to over 30 out of a ratings complement of around 90; hence the devaluation of the rank by the sheer weight of numbers.

The anti U-boat course having finished, the squadron was alive with rumours about the next move and these multiplied when the aircraft were handed over to workshops and orders received to pack kit. Then, surprisingly, we were given two days leave which meant, for most, just local leave. The day after returning from leave, on March 1, the squadron took the train to Larne, the ferry to Stranraer, and the train again to Liverpool; the journey lasting 20 hours. There was much futile discussion, during our coach ride from the station to the Port of Liverpool, about our possible destination but it was soon settled when we boarded SS *Strathnaver*, a 20,000 ton passenger liner of the Pacific and Orient Line - it had to be the Far East. It was now almost a week since we had packed our kit and been given a small kitbag for holding sufficient gear to last us for a few days, by which time our main kit would be available to us. In the event, we did not see our main kitbags again until we arrived in Ceylon, a month later!

* * * *

Returning from home leave, 846 Squadron continued working up at Hatston for the next two months transferring to RNAS Grimsetter at the end of September when it was displaced by the arrival of the squadrons from USS *Ranger* which had joined the Home Fleet at Scapa.

Soon after arriving there, the squadron was involved in what, at the time, appeared to be somewhat of a debacle but , in retrospect, it can now be seen as a unique event. On September 26, a report was received from an RAF reconnaissance patrol that a German warship was preparing to put to sea from its Norwegian base. The warship was thought to be the *Lützow*, formerly the pocket battleship *Deutschland*, and it would be in range for Avengers to make a torpedo attack.

As it happened 845 Squadron, which had been stationed at Hatston for the past two months, was on leave until the 28th. However, 832 Squadron, which had just returned from the Pacific on *Victorious*, had just flown in to Hatston but without most of its squadron personnel who had gone on leave direct from *Victorious*. The compromise solution to the dilemma was to use all available 832 aircrew supplemented by observers and TAGs from 846 Squadron. It was also decided to fly first to Sumburgh, in the Shetlands, where the Avengers would be refuelled and pick up an RAF fighter escort of Beaufighters.

On that basis, the strike was planned for early on the 27th, 846 aircrew having been taken to Hatston from Grimsetter. John Minards, an 846 TAG, with his observer, S/Lt. Warwick Taylor, was on the strike.

> 'We took off around 0700 to fly to Sumburgh, a flight of some forty minutes, and on arrival were given breakfast. Afterwards, we attended a briefing at which it appeared that an RAF Beaufighter squadron was to be our escort for the trip. In the meantime, our Avengers had been refuelled and at 1210 we took off, circling the field while waiting for our fighter escort to join us. With two

Beaufighters airborne, the third ground-looped and hit a bowser thus delaying the others from taking off. As time was of the essence, it was decided to press on with the two fighters as escort but, after a short time, they returned to base leaving us unescorted. Nevertheless, the squadron flew on to the Norwegian coast where, after a fruitless search of the target area, we turned for home. Landing at Sumburgh, after a flight of 3 hours and 20 minutes, we had a short break, while refuelling took place, and then flew back to Hatston arriving at 1830. The frantic events of the past 24 hours had left me tired and weary and I was ready for an early night, leaving the inquest into the whole affair for another day.'

With hindsight, it can be seen that the attempted strike was a recipe for disaster. If the German warship had been found, it would most probably have had air protection from the shore-based fighter squadrons and the unescorted Avengers would have been easy targets. The operation was unique in that few, if any, torpedo attacks by FAA Avengers were attempted during the war.

In October, the squadron commenced anti-submarine training at RNAS Macrihanish, followed by a month at RNAS Maydown, Northern Ireland, before returning to Macrihanish at the beginning of December when a flight of four Wildcat fighters joined. Finally, at the start of 1944, 846 embarked on CVE *Tracker*, the aircraft flying aboard on January 4. The working-up programme with the ship was completed expeditiously but the squadron suffered the loss of one crew when the wing of its Avenger collapsed in a glide-bombing exercise; the TAG was Leading Airman R.F. Gates.

After home leave, 846 returned to *Tracker*, which sailed from the Clyde on February 13 to escort Convoy OS68/KMS 42 to Gibraltar in company with the CVE *Biter*. The passage was uneventful apart from isolated sightings of German aircraft which were driven off by the Wildcats. One Avenger ditched on take-off but the crew was picked up by the attendant escort vessel. After a week's stop-over, *Tracker* and *Biter* sailed for the UK, covering Convoy OS70/

KMS 44. One of the escorts, the Flower Class corvette *Asphodel*, was sunk by *U-575*, but searches by 846 Avengers failed to discover the attacker. The rest of the voyage was quiet and the *Tracker* steamed up the Clyde on March 12.

* * * *

On September 26, 832 aircraft flew into Hatston with few back-seat aircrew aboard as most squadron personnel had gone on leave when *Victorious* docked at Greenock. However, on the 27th, the squadron was involved in an attempted torpedo strike on a German warship - described elsewhere - before the pilots were allowed to go on leave.

In mid-October, 832 Squadron returned from leave to RNAS Hatston where they re-equipped, with TBF-1 Avengers replacing their USN Avengers with which they had been originally equipped. At that time, 845 Squadron was also stationed at Hatston and, for the next nine months, the activities of the two squadrons were to follow a similar pattern, culminating in their joint operations from *Illustrious* in May, 1944.

832 began an intensive flying programme part of which was connected with flight trials and testing of their new Avengers, of which one ended its short service life on November 16 when taking part in a dummy attack on units of the Home Fleet. The weather was far from good, with snow showers sweeping the area, when 845 took off for a mock night attack on the cruiser *Gambia*. Encountering a snowstorm, the squadron was unable to maintain formation and, having separated, had difficulty in re-assembling and so the exercise was abandoned. A short time later, 832 Squadron also took off, for a similar exercise, with the battleships *Howe* and *Duke of York* and, as the squadron went in search of its target, TAG, George Smith had little idea of what fate had in store for him and his crew that night.

'As we approached the target area. I could see the two ships illuminated by a curtain of flares dropped by aircraft in advance of the main body of the squadron. After manoeuvring for position, we dived down, made our dummy attack and pulled away to re-form for the return to base.

However, as we circled to rejoin the rest of the planes we were engulfed in cloud and decided to proceed independently. After a time, on our homeward course, I was sitting in the turret, relaxing after the excitement of the attack, when suddenly the engine cut out and the pilot warned us to prepare for ditching. I had just comprehended this ominous news when the engine started again and I breathed a sigh of relief - the thought of that cold dark sea below was daunting. But, alas, the relief was short-lived as the engine cut out again and this time it was for good. As the plane went down, I remember kicking off my flying boots and checking the position of the quick-release handle on the turret escape hatch then, having no time to signal the base, I locked the Morse key down and switched on the transmitter. With the landing lights full on, the plane hit the sea with considerable impact which, in the confines of the turret. I survived without injury, unlike the observer, who was knocked semi-conscious by a blow on the head. With water still rushing past the turret, I quickly got out onto the wing, pulled out the dinghy from its housing and inflated it with the compressed air bottle. In the meantime, the pilot had climbed out of his cockpit and was assisting the observer to get out onto the wing.

'By this time the aircraft was filling rapidly and we were all three in the water, which was exceedingly cold but fortunately fairly calm. Strange to relate, the Avenger's lights were still shining, and from their reflected glow, I saw that the dinghy was floating upside down so I dived beneath and righted it. Having climbed in, I then helped the pilot to drag the dazed observer inboard, and no sooner were we all three safely ensconced than the plane tipped up its tail and slid below the surface with lights still ablaze.

'In the darkness which followed the plane's disappearance, we spotted lights in the distance not more than a mile or so away. Happily, it appeared we had ditched in sight of the shore, so we put all our efforts into paddling in that direction; the exertion helped us to forget the biting cold and misery of our predicament. At last, we were ashore and the pilot and I assisted the observer across the beach to the road beyond; it was at this stage that I regretted my action in disposing of my flying boots, as the rough nature of the ground cut into my unprotected feet as we stumbled across the shore. On the road awaiting us, as if by magic, was an RN ambulance which whisked us off to the sick-bay at Hatston where we spent the night.

'Two days later we were operational again, and when later flying over the spot where it all happened, we realised how fortunate we had been to have come down in a small bay surrounded by typical Orkney hills and crags; the alternative would have been less pleasant. There was no sign of the aircraft, which had obviously gone down in deep water, and so ended the life of Avenger FN899.'

832 moved to RNAS Macrihanish at the beginning of December and stayed there for two months, apart from a week's break at RNAS Maydown to attend the anti U-boat course. At Macrihanish, the emphasis was on anti-submarine bombing exercises interspersed with some patrols at sea. Then, as in the case of 845, the squadron found itself on the way to Liverpool to board the SS *Strathnaver* for passage to Port Said and from there SS *Aronda* to Colombo.

* * * *

Over the next six months, while working up, 848 was subject to continual moves, first to Orkney, at Grimsetter and Hatston, then Macrihanish, followed by Maydown and Eglington in N. Ireland. Furthermore, squadron detachments were sent to Gosport and Macrihanish. It was at this time, that, by a strange coincidence, the squadron suffered the loss of two crews on the same day but operating from different bases. On 11th April, Avenger JZ125 took off at 2214 from Eglington for a night navigation exercise over the sea to the north but failed to return; Leading Airman E.H. Plain was the TAG. On the same date, Avenger FN878, operating from Macrihanish, crashed into the sea at 1648 one mile off Carradale Point, cause unknown. Leading Airman J. Reed was the TAG of the crew.

On 20th April, 848 was assigned to Coastal Command at RAF Manston, Kent, for operations in the Channel.

* * * *

849 Squadron disembarked at the RAF base at Speke, Liverpool, moving to RNAS Grimsetter in the Orkneys, where it spent three months working up. Then, in the middle of February, 1944, it went to RNAS Maydown, Northern Ireland, for the two-week Anti-Submarine Course, transferring to nearby RNAS Eglington for the next five weeks, to practice what had been learned on the Course. Finally, 849 was assigned to operational service with Coastal Command, joining 850 Squadron at RAF Perranporth on 20th April.

* * * *

Returning to RNAS Macrihanish after leave, 852 started a two month period of working up, interrupted by two weeks at RNAS Maydown for the anti-submarine course. Back at Macrihanish, the squadron lost its first crew when, in bad visibility, their aircraft flew into a hillside north of Carradale, on Kintyre; Leading Airman A.G. Winder was the TAG.

In July, the squadron re-embarked on *Nabob* for working up prior to major operations the following month; during this time, there was a second aircraft loss with fatal casualties. On a night exercise, one Avenger crashed into the sea after taking a wave-off from the batsman when approaching to land. Although the crash was near the *Nabob* and rescue vessels were at hand, the aircraft was carrying live depth charges, which exploded killing the Observer and TAG, PO (A) B.K. Blissett; the pilot amazingly survived, although badly injured.

* * * *

Returning to Macrihanish after taking leave, 853 Squadron moved to RNAS Maydown, Northern Ireland, for an anti-submarine course which sought to acquaint air-crews with the latest tactics for defeating the U-boat menace. The training consisted of classroom lectures supplemented by day and night flying exercises in conjunction with escort vessels and submarines. The squadron then returned to Macrihanish where they undertook a full programme of low-level attacks on fixed targets using practice bombs. There were also practice dives on surfaced submarines and, finally, the dropping of live depth charges in the sea.

The squadron was to join *Tracker*, but there was a delay of a few weeks before they embarked, during which time their complement of Avengers was reduced to nine but supplemented by a flight of Wildcat fighters. On 12th September, the aircraft flew aboard the ship in the Firth of Clyde and, over the next month, there followed a hectic period of working up. As well as the inevitable deck landings, by day and night, Avengers, each paired with a Wildcat, practised attacking a towed target, both firing their front guns and the Avengers dropping practice bombs. The final day of working up was performed under the scrutiny of Admiral Lister, Flag Officer Carrier Training, who came aboard for the occasion. Presumably, all being to his satisfaction, the ship sailed for Scapa on 14th October; the squadron having been unexpectedly increased to eleven Avengers.

∗ ∗ ∗ ∗

At Macrihanish, 856 undertook anti-submarine training with day and night bombing exercises. On one of the night exercises, dropping flares, an aircraft crashed into the sea, east of Campbeltown, while executing a low-level turn; Leading Airman J.B. Watson was the TAG of the crew which was lost. A few days later, another tragedy occurred, when four of the squadron armourers were killed and two injured following an explosion in the bomb store. At the end of July, the squadron moved to RNAS Maydown, Northern Ireland, for the anti-U-boat course, after which six aircraft, with crews, were detached to RNAS Hatston on secondment to 846 and 852 Squadrons for Operation GOODWOOD - described elsewhere. The rest of the squadron went to RNAS Eglington, Northern Ireland, for the Convoy

Escort Course.

On September 8, a flight of four Wildcats joined the squadron, at which time the number of Avengers was reduced to nine. A few days later, the squadron embarked on the escort carrier *Premier* and immediately began an intensive period of working up in the Firth of Clyde, with both day and night exercises. During these, in a period of three weeks, nine Avengers were damaged, some beyond repair, in a series of deck landing accidents. The Flag Officer Carrier Training came aboard during October 11 and 12 for his final inspection, after which the ship put in at Greenock where the squadron went ashore for 8 days leave.

First wire again

CHANNEL OPERATIONS

As part of the preparations for the invasion of Europe, a number of FAA squadrons were put under the control of Coastal Command; five of these were Avenger squadrons which, in the second quarter of 1944, were based at RAF airfields along the south coast. For this purpose, three General Reconnaissance Wings were formed to which the squadrons were attached; 848 joined No.155 at Manston in April, 849 and 850 joined No.156 at Perranporth also in April, while 854 and 855 joined No. 157 at Hawkinge in May. With their aircraft painted with the black and white stripes of the invasion forces, they carried out numerous and varied operations, off the coasts of France, Belgium and Holland, for the next five months by which time, with the invasion securely established, their services were no longer required. The squadrons had, in the meantime, returned to FAA control in August.

* * * *

848 Squadron arrived at RAF Manston on 20th April for operations in the Channel under the control of No. 16 Group, Coastal Command. As with the other FAA squadrons, operations comprised anti-shipping strikes off the enemy coasts and convoy patrols in the Channel. Sam Hodgkinson, a TAG with 848, recalls that patrols were fairly lengthy, some lasting for nearly five hours. On May 19, one crew was lost when its aircraft failed to return from a patrol between Flushing and Helde; the TAG was Leading Airman G.G. Bream. In the middle of June, 848 moved to RAF Thorney Island to continue operations but returned to FAA control on August 24 when it transferred to RNAS

Lee-on-Solent. After completion of the Channel operations, with Coastal Command, 848 was sent to join the *Formidable* for operations with the Pacific Fleet. The squadron had only been aboard *Formidable* for a short time, at Rosyth, when some of the TAGs had a sharp reminder of the difference between serving on an RAF station and an RN fleet carrier. Four of them were unfortunate to be found on the mess-deck during the course of the First Lieutenant's rounds and were immediately accused of skulking away to avoid work duties. For the past few months, operating from RAF stations, TAGs, as aircrew, were not expected to undertake other than their flying duties, but that excuse cut no ice with the First Lieutenant and he forthwith detailed them off to help loading ship. They were given the task of securing crates of Corsair drop tanks on storage racks on the hangar deckhead some 15 feet up. The crate, with one TAG at each corner, was raised by the simple expedient of the attachment of a wire cable, threaded through a pulley attached to the deckhead, and the other end connected to an aircraft-towing vehicle. Unfortunately for the TAGs, the operator doing the towing failed to stop when the crate reached the deckhead, the cable snapped, and they, together with the crate were sent crashing to the steel deck below. Two TAGS suffered broken limbs and left the squadron, while the other two spent a spell in sickbay. Sam Hodgkinson, one of the latter two, still finds it ironical that this was the only injury he suffered in his service with 848; surviving operations in the Channel and in the Pacific without a scratch.

On September 16th, *Formidable* sailed for the Far East, with 848 flying anti-submarine patrols to Gibraltar, where the ship developed engine trouble and remained there for three months while repairs were carried out. In the meantime, 848 aircraft were flown to Dekheila, an RNAS base in Egypt, where they were joined by the rest of the squadron, who travelled by sea. Here, the squadron, which had been increased to 21 aircraft in September, continued with their working up. During this time, on November 16, Leading Airman O.L. Cribb was killed in an accident.

At the end of January, 1945, *Formidable* reached Alexandria, 848 re-embarked and the ship sailed for Australia, reaching Sydney on March 10. After taking on stores, the ship sailed for Manus and then Leyte, joining the BPF on April 13.

* * * *

849 Squadron started operations in the Channel from RAF Perranporth under the control of No. 19 Group, Coastal Command, moving to RAF St. Eval in early August. It returned to FAA control two weeks later and transferred to RNAS Lee-on-Solent before moving to Belfast to board CVE *Rajah* sailing for Ceylon on September 9.

* * * *

In the second half of April, 850 Squadron flew in to RAF Perranporth for operations in the Channel with No 19 Group, Coastal Command. On 24 July, in operations off Guernsey, the squadron sank one merchant ship and damaged another. At the end of the month, it was transferred to Northern Ireland where it continued with anti-submarine patrols with No. 15 Group of Coastal Command until it was disbanded on Christmas Eve 1944.

* * * *

854 Squadron, after disembarkation leave, returned to RNAS Macrihanish on 19th May but soon moved south to RAF Hawkinge to commence operations in the Channel as part of No. 157(GR) Wing. There it carried out anti-submarine patrols and convoy escort duties by day and anti-shipping patrols, off the French coast, by night. After only a week, on June 7, one of its Avengers failed to return from a patrol in the Pas-de-Calais area; Leading Airman L.C. Green was the TAG of that crew. At the time, the Germans were launching their flying-bombs from bases across the Channel and Hawkinge, lying under their flight path, had numerous anti-aircraft batteries in the area which put up tremendous barrages in attempts to shoot the Doodlebugs down before they penetrated inland. This meant that aircraft going on patrol had to fly along a safe corridor leading through

the barrages - an unnerving experience to begin and end a patrol! On one occasion, a squadron plane was able to shoot down a flying-bomb when it came within range of the turret-gun; the TAG, Leading Airman F.C. Shirmer, was mentioned in dispatches for his achievement. In July, the squadron started night Rover patrols and used radar not only to locate the target but also to deliver the attack in those cases where bad visibility would otherwise have prevented it. On July 14, TAG, Jack Gardiner, took off on two patrols during the day which had to be aborted because of the bad visibility out in the Channel despite the weather forecasts at the operations briefing which predicted clear skies. It was some days later that the reason for the discrepancy was established - it was the smoke rising from the bombardment of Caen, some hundred miles away across the Channel! In early August, 854 was transferred to Thorney Island, where it continued operations for a few more weeks before boarding CVE *Activity* bound for the Far East; its aircraft were left ashore.

* * * *

At the end of May, 855 joined 854 at Hawkinge, and after familiarisation with its new surroundings, commenced operations with daylight anti-shipping patrols ranging from Cherbourg in the south to the Friesian Islands in the north. Night bombing missions on shipping also began, but owing to the lack of night flying facilities at Hawkinge, the squadrons moved, first to Thorney Island near Portsmouth then to Docking near the north Norfolk coast. Two of the TAGs serving on the squadron during this time were Herb Beardshaw and Bill Campbell who trained on the same TAG Course in Canada. Bill's log shows that the night Rover patrols were of three to four hours duration and a variety of shipping, from E-Boats to 6,000 ton merchantmen were bombed and strafed. Flak was a constant danger and the aircraft often sustained damage. Bill recalls one occasion when, dropping down from the turret after an attack, he found, to his great surprise, a gaping hole in the fuselage, large enough to climb through. His mind had been so fully occupied with the attack that he had no recollection of the plane being badly hit, but luckily the damage did not affect its flying capacity and it returned safely to fight another day. However, all crews were not so fortunate and 855 suffered more losses than the other four Avenger squadrons in total. At Hawkinge, on successive days in July, two aircraft failed to return from patrol; the TAGs lost were Leading Airman S.W. Norman and PO(A) H.C. Selby. Another loss was at Thorney Island on 4th September when an Avenger failed to return from patrol; PO(A) G.A. Stephenson was the TAG lost. Although few in number, these losses represented a quarter of the squadron complement in four months of operations, a not inconsiderable sacrifice.

By the middle of October, 855's services were no longer required and so the squadron moved to RNAS Macrihanish where, a few days later, it was disbanded on the 19th.

* * * *

Of the five Avenger squadrons taking part in the Channel operations during the summer months of 1944, three were sent to the Far East to participate in the sustained fighting with the Japanese while the other two squadrons, 850 and 855, were disbanded. It is interesting to speculate on the reasons for these decisions, as the effect upon the personnel of those squadrons was so markedly different. The majority were committed to some of the most bitter fighting of the war at sea while the fate of the others was left to the vagaries of the drafting system.

* * * *

846, on *Tracker,* was looking forward to its coming role in the Channel operations. Working up commenced immediately and all aircraft were painted with the black and white recognition stripes of the invasion forces. The *Tracker* was part of the fleet responsible for patrolling the South West Approaches to prevent any enemy warships approaching the established beachheads but little was seen of the enemy. However, on the night of June 10, *Tracker* collided with the Canadian frigate *Teme* which crossed its bows unexpectedly while chasing an enemy contact. *Teme*, although badly damaged, was taken in tow by another escort vessel and reached the UK safely but sadly four of her crew were killed in the collision. As *Tracker* was also damaged, she withdrew from the area, sailing to Belfast for inspection of damage. 846 aircraft flew ashore to RAF Limavady for three weeks before embarking on the escort carrier *Trumpeter*. After working up in the Firth of Clyde, the ship sailed for Scapa prior to taking part in mine-laying operations off the coast of Norway.

On draft

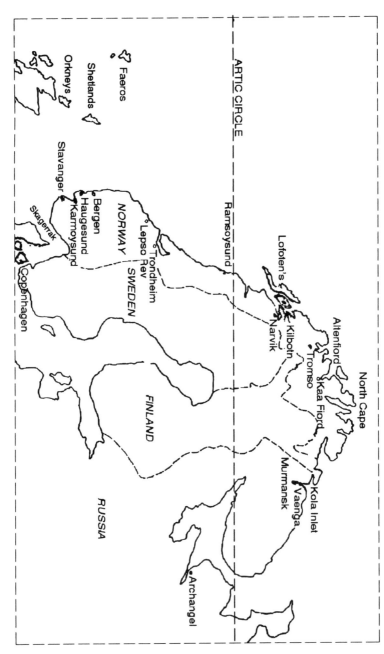

NORTHERN WATERS

NORTHERN WATERS

On March 25, *Tracker* sailed from Tail-of-the-Bank for Scapa from where, three days later, she sailed to join the Russian Convoy JW58 consisting of 48 merchant ships. Air cover was to be provided by the two carriers, *Tracker* and *Activity*, with 846's 12 Avengers and 7 Wildcats on the former and 3 Swordfish and 7 Wildcats on the latter. In addition, the convoy was to be accompanied by two escort groups, twenty destroyers, and a US cruiser, all under the command of Admiral Dalrymple-Hamilton in the cruiser *Diadem*; altogether a most impressive escort. A day later, the Home Fleet put to sea as two distinct task forces; Force I was to shadow convoy JW58 for the first part of its passage and Force II was to launch an attack, with Barracuda bombers, on the *Tirpitz* in Altenfjord. This attack, code-named Operation TUNGSTEN, was designed to keep the *Tirpitz* out of action, so removing the threat to Russian convoys, posed by its presence in the area. In the event, the two Forces met and re-grouped on April 2 and, on the following morning, two strikes by Barracudas succeeded in inflicting serious damage on the *Tirpitz*, putting it out of action for some months.

In the meantime, Convoy JW58 was making good progress despite the appearance of shadowing aircraft and the detection of U-boats in the vicinity. On March 29, Captain Walker's escort sank *U-961* and, a few days later, *U-360* was sunk by the destroyer *Keppel*. Meanwhile, the Avengers of 846 operated with Wildcats to deliver co-ordinated attacks on the U-boats, the fighter strafing while the Avenger dropped its depth charges. The practice was to have one Avenger and one Wildcat at stand-by on deck to be launched whenever a U-boat contact was signalled by the escort vessels. Alternatively, patrols were made by the two aircraft, thereby reducing the response time for reaching the target area. In all, six U-boats were sighted and attacked by aircraft during the outward trip but the first confirmed success by 846 was the sinking of *U-355* in conjunction with the escort vessel *Beagle*. The second was the sinking of *U-288*, first sighted by a Swordfish from *Activity*. On arrival of the Avenger and Wildcat, all three aircraft attacked the luckless U-boat which was seen to blow up and sink. For these successes two 846 TAGs were subsequently awarded a DSM and an MID.

However, this period of success was not without its misfortune when, on April 1, *Tracker* was threatened by an emergency not of the enemy's making, which could have caused serious damage and casualties aboard ship. During a morning patrol, an 846 Avenger sighted and attacked a U-boat but found that the depth-charges had failed to drop. Marking the spot where the U-boat had dived, the Avenger returned to the ship, reporting that three of the four depth-charges had subsequently been released. The aircraft then came into land but, despite the frenzied signals of the Batsman, crashed into the round-down. Almost immediately, the petrol tanks exploded and flames enveloped the plane which had the engine embedded in the round-down, the tail resting on the stern, and the port wing supported by the Bofors gun. Fire Control Parties were soon tackling the fire, but there was the more serious question of the fourth depth-charge left in the aircraft and, also, those stored on the ship immediately below where the fire was raging. The Torpedo Officer managed to clear the latter, but it was impossible to do anything about the other one except put out the fire before it exploded.

By now, the crew of the Avenger had somehow managed to escape to the deck below but the pilot, S/Lt.(A) A.E. Ballentyne RNVR, was a mass of flames as he stumbled into the hangar and, although members of the Ship's Company quickly extinguished the flames, he died soon afterwards. The observer, S/Lt. (A) K. D. Callaway RNVR, and the TAG, L/A G. E. Hearn, were not seriously injured and survived.

The fire had now consumed the fuselage of the plane so that it broke up and the engine fell away, transferring the centre of the fire from the flight deck to the deck below. The ammunition in the aircraft and that in the Bofors gun-locker started to explode, adding to the danger for those fighting the fire. But for all on the ship, there remained the constant thought of that live depth-charge which might explode at any second. Fortunately, events proved that the fourth depth-charge was not aboard and the efforts of all concerned in the emergency succeeded in putting out the fire after 15 minutes. During that short period, the safety of the ship had been threatened and with it, perhaps, that of the convoy. That evening S/Lt. Ballentyne was buried at sea, with the ceremony attended by the Ship's Company, in the driving snow.

On April 4, the convoy arrived at Kola Inlet, without losing a ship while inflicting the loss of four U-boats and four shadowing aircraft upon the enemy - a unique achievement. On the return passage, Convoy RA58, comprising 36 merchantmen, had a relatively quiet time, with only a few tentative attempts by the enemy to attack the ships. On April 11, the two carriers left the convoy to return to Scapa, where 846 flew ashore to Hatston while the *Tracker* sailed for Belfast for repairs arising from the Avenger crash on the round-down.

On April 28, 846 re-embarked on *Tracker* for service in the Atlantic, sweeping the Western Approaches before the arrival of an incoming convoy. In the event, heavy gales prevented flying for most of the time; in fact, the weather deteriorated to the extent that no-one was allowed on the flight deck and the stand-by Avenger secured on the after-end was blown overboard. When the time came for *Tracker* to turn for home, there was some general anxiety regarding the effect of the heavy seas when the ship was broadside on to the waves. It became known that a CVE was designed to recover from a roll of up to 52 degrees and so, in the squadron workshop, a makeshift protractor was set up to measure the roll when it occurred. As the ship came broadside on to the seas, the weighted string swung across the scale, first showing 20 degrees, then 30, and not until over 40 did the string start creeping back to the vertical. The relief was audible! The only success was achieved by the No 2 Escort Group which sank *U-473* on May 5. Returning to Scapa, the squadron then moved to RNAS Macrihanish until rejoining *Tracker* on June 3 for Operation NEPTUNE, the invasion of Normandy - described in a previous chapter.

For Operation OFFSPRING, described elsewhere, 846 on *Trumpeter*, operated with 852 on *Nabob*, supported by other units of the Home Fleet. In the second strike of the day, August 10, one of the Avengers of 846 was hit by flak and failed to return. PO(A) J.H. Ashton was the TAG of the crew and was subsequently mentioned in despatches for his part in the raid. The next day, the *Trumpeter* was back in Scapa where it was soon involved in preparations for Operation GOODWOOD.

Before sailing for Operation GOODWOOD, described elsewhere, *Trumpeter*, with 846 aboard, took part in the Fleet rehearsal for the operation at Loch Eriboll. It was to be a major strike on the *Tirpitz* by the Home Fleet, with *Trumpeter* and *Nabob* providing the Avenger squadrons for laying mines to seal off possible escape routes to the sea. The operation had been planned to cover a seven-day period starting August 22, but, for the two escort carriers, it finished on the first day, when *Nabob* was torpedoed. Alf Austin, TAG of one of three crews of 856 Avenger Squadron, which had joined 846 for the strike, recalls the occasion.

'I happened to be in my aircraft waiting to take-off when *Nabob* was torpedoed but on the subsequent patrol of three and a half hours duration, we did not spot any U-boat.'

Trumpeter escorted *Nabob* back to Scapa arriving there on August 27.

In a couple of weeks, *Trumpeter* had sailed again for a mine-laying operation, this time, in Aarumsund Fjord. In addition to 846 Avengers were six of 852 whose crews had been recalled from leave, granted after the torpedoing of the *Nabob*. Operation BEGONIA was carried out on September 12 and all aircraft returned safely, although the aircraft of 846's CO was hit by flak and, as a result of the damage sustained, he had to make a one-wheeled deck landing, which was accomplished without injury to the crew. Returning to Scapa on the 13th, the squadron flew ashore to Hatston, staying there until the 23rd when it re-embarked for Operation TENABLE. Owing to bad weather, the operation was cancelled after a week at sea and *Trumpeter* returned to Scapa where 846 went ashore to Hatston.

On October 12, it was back to *Trumpeter* again for two operations in just over a week. The first, Operation LYCIDES, was the laying of mines at Ramsoysund, north of Trondheim, on the 15th, while the second, Operation HARDY, covered both mine-laying and shipping strikes at Lepsorer on the 24th. Then it was back to Scapa, where 846 went ashore to Hatston for three weeks, followed by a week at RNAS Macrihanish before re-embarking on *Trumpeter* again on November 23.

During the next two months, *Trumpeter*, with 846 aboard, sailed from Scapa on six occasions for operations in Norwegian waters, in most of these, 846 was joined by 856, operating from *Premier*. Descriptions of the raids are given elsewhere. On February 6, *Trumpeter*, needing a refit, sailed for the Clyde where she remained until March 2 when, after trials, she returned to Scapa to escort the Russian Convoy JW65.

Convoy JW65 sailed for Russia in mid-March with escort carriers *Campania* and *Trumpeter*; the former having twelve Swordfish and seven Wildcats and the latter eight Avengers of 846 and eight Wildcats. No contact was made with the enemy until approaching the Kola Inlet where two merchantmen were torpedoed by U-boats. The return Convoy, RA65, sailed after two days and reached the UK without loss. For squadron personnel, these convoys meant extremely long hours working in the hangar, to maintain aircraft serviceability for patrols during the long daylight hours. Ground crews, working below decks, did not see much daylight, with the result that the combination of long hours and lack of sunlight gave a greyish pallor to the features. This condition was referred to as the "Tracker Tan", named after their first experience of the condition, on their first Russian Convoy aboard the *Tracker*. Fortunately, the pallor soon disappeared when exposed to the sunlight.

On May 1, *Trumpeter*, with escort carriers *Queen* and *Searcher*, sailed for Operation JUDGEMENT, a strike on shipping in the U-boat harbour of Kilbotn, where the target for 846 was to be the 5,000 ton depot ship, *Black Watch*. The operation proved to be an outstanding success, with two depot ships and a U-boat sunk; a detailed description is given elsewhere. One Avenger of 846 was hit by flak and failed to return, the TAG being Leading Airman P.B. Mansfield. This was to be the last FAA offensive action in Europe.

A few days later, with the imminent collapse of Germany, *Trumpeter* joined *Queen* and *Searcher* again, on this occasion, for Operation CLEAVER, the surrender of German naval forces in Copenhagen. 846's role was to provide anti-submarine patrols for the security of the fleet, including the 50th Mine-Sweeping Flotilla which was clearing a passage for the fleet to enter Copenhagen harbour. This done, the carriers returned to Scapa on May 10 when 846 disembarked from *Trumpeter* for the last time.

For the few remaining months of its existence, 846 Squadron served on land stations in Scotland until, on September 22, at RNAS Macrihanish, it was set up as a trials unit and renumbered 751, which, the next month, was disbanded.

* * * *

On 9th August, *Nabob*, in company with *Trumpeter*, the fleet carrier *Indefatigable*, cruiser squadron, and destroyer escort, sailed for the coast of Norway for a major mine-laying operation by the Avengers of 852 and 846. The next day, 852 took off at 1300 and mines were laid in Lepsoyren Channel and Haarhamsfjord with little opposition, but in the second strike, in the evening, when further mines were laid, the flak was more intense. For the operation, *Indefatigable* provided the fighter cover and carried out bombing and strafing attacks on shipping and ground installations. One of the TAGs on 852, Arthur Stocker, who was sitting in the turret of his Avenger, flying low as it left the target area, recalls an odd incident.

'One thing which sticks in my memory was the sight of German soldiers running across a parade ground, with one of them minus his pants!'

The operation was judged a great success; the 47 mines laid represented one of the largest mine-laying operations by the Home Fleet and would constitute a serious obstacle to the free movement of enemy shipping in the area. Additionally, the fighters had caused considerable damage to hangars, warehouses, radar stations, barracks, and shipping. On the return to Scapa, *Nabob* put in at Rosyth to take on board a supply of special mines for future operations.

The next operation for 852, on *Nabob*, was titled GOODWOOD and involved another attack on the *Tirpitz* by the Home Fleet, including three fleet carriers, battleship, two cruisers and destroyer escort, together with an assault group comprising the escort carriers *Nabob* and *Trumpeter* with frigate escort. The latter's role in the attack was the subsidiary one of laying mines to seal off the route by which *Tirpitz* might reach the open sea. The operation was planned to take place in four phases from August 22 to 29, but bad weather on the first day caused the first attack by Barracuda squadrons to be aborted. At around 1730 on that day, *Nabob*'s part in the operation was ended when she was struck by a torpedo fired by *U-354*. The explosion ripped a huge hole in the starboard side aft and *Nabob* started to settle by the stern. The Fleet sailed on, leaving the two escort carriers and its escort vessels to cope with the situation which, less than ten minutes later, seriously deteriorated when one of the circling frigates, *Bickerton*, was also hit by a torpedo, perhaps meant for *Nabob*. The frantic efforts of the crew on the carrier were now directed to shoring up the bulkheads adjacent to the damaged hull, moving aircraft forward to lighten the load on the stern and getting the engines working. Around 2100, all personnel not required for working the ship were transferred to the escort vessels to join the surviving members of *Bickerton*'s crew who had been rescued from the badly-damaged frigate, which was later sunk by other escorts. By this time, the *Nabob* had got under way and, with her over-manned escorts, started to make slow progress towards Scapa, some five days steaming away. However, danger was still following them, as indicated on the radar screens. Fortunately, two aircrews from 852 were still aboard and, despite the alarming angle of the flight deck, it was decided to fly two Avengers off, using the booster. The first to go was the CO's crew, followed by a second, and the presence of these two aircraft forced the U-Boat to dive and stay submerged, thus preventing it from tracking the *Nabob* and, after a period, losing contact. The recovery of the aircraft posed a more difficult problem than the take-off, owing to the angle of the flight deck and the ship's slow speed. Nevertheless, the first landed without mishap, but by the time that the CO was ready to land the ship was shrouded in mist and he had to make a blind approach, hitting the sloping deck and crashing into the aircraft parked forward, which stopped his progress; a crash barrier of sorts!

From thenceforth, *Nabob*, with *Trumpeter* and escorts in attendance, proceeded unhindered for the remaining 1,000 mile passage to Scapa, surviving two periods of stormy weather. A remarkable achievement of seamanship by the Canadian-manned escort carrier commanded by the Captain, Horatio Nelson Ley. Unfortunately, *Nabob* was considered too badly damaged for repair and did not sail again during the war. A worse fate awaited *U-354* which, within three days of its successful strikes, was sunk by a Swordfish from *Vindex*.

At Scapa, 852 disembarked from the escort vessels which had carried most of their members to safety; a number were killed when the torpedo struck the carrier near the FAA messes. The survivors were sent to RNAS Lee-on-Solent for re-kitting before going on leave and, on the journey south, stopped at Carlisle for a meal. TAG, Arthur Stocker, recalls the occasion.

'We marched from the station to the British Restaurant
and you can imagine what an ill-dressed group of matelots
we looked, but to our surprise, the people of Carlisle cheered
us all the way - I will never forget it.'

After a few days leave, the squadron was recalled to the *Trumpeter* for further mine-laying and shipping strikes off the coast of Norway and, at the end of September, 4 crews were transferred to *Fencer*, another escort carrier, for similar operations. However, the squadron's days were numbered and on 17th October it was disbanded. Most of the TAGs were sent to RNAS Lee-on-Solent and some, like Arthur Stocker, found themselves drafted to 820 Squadron on *Indefatigable*, bound for the Far East.

* * * *

On 21st October, 1944, *Tracker*, with 853 Squadron aboard, sailed from Scapa to join convoy JW 61 to Russia. It was a large convoy of 62 merchantmen protected by *Tracker*, *Nairana* and *Vindex*, the first such convoy to have three carriers, with the cruiser *Dido* and three escort groups. The merchant ships were formed up in a hollow rectangle, leaving the space in the centre for the carriers to operate. The carriers took it in turns to be duty ship for an eight-hour shift, but the *Tracker* always had the daytime duty while the other two carriers, with Swordfish squadrons aboard, operated the night-shifts.

The Avenger patrols, usually launched by catapult, were made by two aircraft, 50 miles ahead of the convoy and extending to 25 miles either side of the line of advance. On the third day out, U-boats were detected by radio direction finding and as a result further Avengers were launched on close-up patrols. During the morning, a U-boat was sighted on the surface, and when it dived the Avenger dropped an Oscar, an acoustic homing depth charge, which failed to explode. A later enquiry into the failure revealed that the depth charge had been dropped unarmed owing to a fault in the arming device in the aircraft. There was great disappointment in the squadron. The next day the convoy reached the Kola Inlet, where the merchantmen proceeded to Murmansk to discharge cargo while the escorts anchored at Vaenga Bay.

Owing to reports that U-boats were in the vicinity of the Inlet, the escort put to sea a day early, swamping the area with ships and aircraft to force them to submerge. *Tracker* sailed on 2nd November, followed by the convoy in the evening. On the first day, 853 Avengers continued their patrols, sighting a U-boat on the surface, which dived before an attack was possible; one aircraft was badly damaged when landing on. The weather was very variable with winds and visibility changing rapidly from one extreme to the other while a heavy swell caused the carrier decks to move alarmingly. The onset of very light winds meant that the Avengers were deck-bound on two days and the Swordfish had to undertake both day and night shifts. Soon they were back at Scapa with the satisfaction of knowing that the first operation had been a total success, with no ship being lost. *Tracker* soon left for the Clyde, where the squadron flew off to Macrihanish for leave, and on their return to the ship had almost immediately to fly off again, this time, to Hatston. *Tracker*, having just finished ten successful operations, would be sailing westward to the Pacific to join the Carrier Transport Service.

At Hatston, weather permitting, the squadron was back to its usual routines of anti-submarine bombing and deck landing practice, although a new element in the training was the introduction of glide bombing. After leave over Christmas and the New year, the squadron learned that the next move would be to the newly-commissioned *Queen*, another escort carrier.

Having embarked on *Queen*, the squadron was now faced with yet more training but, in this instance, it was as much for the benefit of the ship as for themselves. During the first two weeks of February, weather permitting, there was flying each day and occasionally at night also. Landing Avengers on an escort carrier at night was risky enough in the best of conditions, but during winter in the Firth of Clyde it was a perilous undertaking. The ship was virtually unlit apart from a single white light of limited directional visibility, dim blue lights along the edges of the flight deck, and the three lights on the batsman, one held in either hand and the third fixed to his chest. On starless nights, the pilots were entirely dependent upon the illuminated figure of the batsman to judge their approach to the ship, and then for his detailed signals to effect a safe landing. Each pilot completed four landings during the two nights exercise and when it was over there was a feeling of satisfaction at the absence of any mishaps. However, this illusion was spoilt when John Barnes, one of the TAGs flying on the exercise, reported to his pilot that one of the blister windows in the lower cabin had been smashed. This brought forth the inevitable question from his pilot as to how he had done it, whereupon John explained that it happened when they had hit the sea. The pilot found this explanation incredulous and so a number of the aircrew went up on deck to examine the damage. On looking into the cabin, they saw a pool of water, which the pilot suggested must have leaked through the turret above. John did not argue the point but merely dipped his finger in the water and, putting it to his lips, murmured, 'Salt rain, Sir?' There was no further argument, just a quiet reflection on how near that crew had come to possible extinction. The plane had been flying with its undercarriage down, which must have hit a wave-top, creating a splash which caused the damage. The blister protruded from the side of the fuselage about six inches and so would take the full force of the sea-water displaced by the impact of the wheel.

The night flying also included mine-laying exercises, one of which the Flag Officer Carrier Training came aboard to watch and then, after more leave for the squadron personnel, the ship sailed for Scapa, where the aircraft complement was changed to 9 Avengers and 8 Wildcats. Flying operations continued, with the ship confined to the Flow itself.

The squadron's next operation, code-named CUPOLA, started on 19th March, 1945, when *Queen* together with carriers *Premier* and *Searcher*, the cruiser *Bellona*, and destroyer escort sailed for Norwegian waters. The aim was daylight mining in the Leads which was undertaken by 856 Squadron Avengers operating from *Premier*, with fighter cover provided by *Searcher*. 853's role was the minor one of anti-submarine patrols, with their Wildcats giving cover for the fleet. Owing to the stormy weather, some damage to aircraft was sustained and the fleet returned to Scapa for replacements.

After two days, *Queen* sailed again, accompanied by the three escort carriers *Searcher, Puncher* and *Nairana*, the cruiser *Dido*, and destroyer escort. The first operation, PREFIX, was to be an attack on enemy shipping by 853 Squadron armed with four 500 lb bombs. However, having reached the target area, the squadron found nothing but empty sea and so, jettisoning their bombs, they turned for home, only to be intercepted by a flight of BF109s from a nearby fighter base. Fortunately, the Wildcats from *Searcher*, flying top cover, swooped down and dispersed the 109s before they could attack the Avengers; all planes returned safely to the ship.

The fleet then withdrew for a day before returning for Operation CAREFREE, which was to be a bombing attack on shipping at Aasborg by the Barracudas of 821 Squadron from *Puncher*. Again, it was not to be, the low cloud ceiling precluded any bombing and so the mission was restricted to strafing by Wildcats. The fleet then returned to Scapa where 853 Squadron flew ashore to Hatston.

For the next few days flying was devoted entirely to glide and dive bombing on the nearby ranges, when the Avenger's deficiency in the latter role was plainly apparent. The build-up of the speed in the dive was such, even with wheels down and bomb bay doors open, as to prevent a sustained angle of dive steep enough to give the accuracy of true dive bombing. Nevertheless, by keeping the altitude of bomb release to the minimum commensurate with safety, between 1,200 and 1,400 feet, good results were obtained.

In early April, the squadron re-embarked on *Queen* which sailed from Scapa as part of a carrier task force sent to attack enemy shipping in Kilbotn, the U-boat harbour near Harstad. However, bad weather intervened and Operation NEWMARKET was aborted; the fleet returned to Scapa, leaving 853 to fly off again to Hatston for yet more bombing practice.

At the end of April, the squadron again flew aboard *Queen* but, on this occasion, things went badly wrong with the final landing. With five Avengers parked ahead of the crash barriers, the last one came in to land, safely hooked a wire, so that the barriers were immediately lowered, when its hook broke away from the tail, so leaving it to plough into the Avengers parked ahead. All six planes were so badly damaged that the next operation had to be postponed while replacements were obtained.

At last, on 1st May, 1945, the fleet, comprising the carriers *Queen, Trumpeter*, and *Searcher*, the cruisers *Norfolk* and *Diadem* and destroyer escort, sailed from Scapa for Operation JUDGEMENT, with the same target as for the cancelled Operation NEWMARKET. The U-boat harbour at Kilbotn was near Harstad, on one of the Lofoten Islands, and the targets were the depot ships *Black Watch* and *Meteor* and the anti-aircraft cruiser *Harald Haarflagger*. 846 Avengers from *Trumpeter* and 853 Avengers from *Queen* were to bomb the two depot ships, while Wildcats from *Searcher* and *Queen* would provide fighter escort and join in the attack by strafing and bombing the AA cruiser.

During the three day passage, crews were fully briefed and on 4th May, at 4pm, when 70 miles from the Norwegian coast, the aircraft started to take to the air. The Avengers, with their 4 x 500lb bomb load, had to be boosted off and so it was 15 minutes before the 44 aircraft were heading for the target at low level to avoid detection by enemy radar. Before reaching the target area, the Avengers climbed to around 4,000 feet, their glide-bombing height, when the enemy flak started to erupt: 846 dived to attack first, followed by 853; bombs being released around 1,500 feet. Then, they made their escape out to sea, forming up loosely against possible enemy fighter attack, but none came. Back aboard, it was found that two planes were missing, one 846 Avenger and one 882 Wildcat. In addition, the CO, whose aircraft had been hit by flak and riddled with shrapnel, was fortunate to get back safely. Senior TAG, Ron Astbury, who was flying with him, sustained a flesh wound and was later awarded the DSM for his part in the attack.

The debriefing assessment of the results of the raid indicated that both depot ships were badly damaged. However, subsequent photographic reconnaissance revealed that both had been sunk, while, in addition, U-boat *U-711*, moored between them, had also been sunk. The 853 target turned out to be the *Karl von Herring*, another depot ship, not the *Meteor*, as first thought. Also, the *Harald Haarflagger* had sustained damage from the Wildcats' onslaught. Although the depot ship, *Black Watch*, was the target for 846 Squadron, which scored a number of hits, it was also bombed by Buck Buchanan, the last 853 pilot to attack. Owing to his target being obscured by the smoke and spray caused by the bombs of previous aircraft, he switched his attack to the *Black Watch*, and an enormous explosion followed, witnessed by another 853 pilot, Jim Spencer. This operation proved to be the last FAA attack in Europe.

Unknown to 853 Squadron at the time, they had only two more operations before they were to be disbanded. From 6th to 10th May, the fleet, with the addition of the carrier *Campania*, covered the operation to open the Skaggerack for a force of HM ships to enter Copenhagen harbour for the surrender of the German naval authorities there. Then, on 14th May, *Queen*, with two destroyers, joined the Russian Convoy JW 67 consisting of 26 merchantmen and 11 escort vessels; this was a necessary precaution against the possibility of a violation of the cease-fire agreement by individual U-boat commanders. For the 6 days passage, 853 flew patrols continuously and entered Kola Inlet without incident. On 23rd May, the last Russian convoy, RA 67, consisting of 25 merchantmen, was escorted back to the UK. *Queen* returned to Greenock, the squadron, flying off for the last time on May 30, bound for Ayr. It would be over 40 years before a squadron reunion took place!

* * * *

On returning from home leave to *Premier*, at Greenock, 856 Squadron undertook more exercises in the Firth of Clyde before proceeding to Scapa Flow in readiness for its first mine-laying operation, code-named HANDFAST. This was carried out on November 20 by nine Avengers and four Wildcats of 856 on *Premier* and twelve Wildcats from the accompanying escort carrier *Pursuer*; the target was the Salhusströmmen Channel, near Haugesund. In such operations, the Avengers had to fly straight and level, in formation, at a given height, from a pre-selected point and drop their mines in a co-ordinated pattern; only precise positioning would effectively block the channel to shipping. In carrying out this manoeuvre, the Avengers were vulnerable to fighter attack, particularly as there was a German air-base at nearby Stavanger. Before reaching the target, one Avenger, with Alf Austin as TAG, was hit by light flak, which shattered the windscreen panels, temporarily blinding the pilot. As a result, they were forced to abort the mission, jettison their mine, and return for an emergency deck landing. Subsequent reconnaissance reports indicated that the operation had been successful in its objective to block the channel to shipping.

The task force returned to Scapa only to join the Home Fleet for further operations off the Norwegian coast but, encountering severe gales, the escort carriers were forced to return to Scapa, where the squadron flew ashore to Hatston. A week later, 856 returned to the *Premier* and prepared for another mine-laying operation at Haugesund, accompanied, on this occasion, by the escort carrier *Trumpeter*. All Wildcats from *Premier* were transferred to *Trumpeter*, while five Avengers of 846 were detached to *Premier*. The task force, comprising *Implacable, Premier, Trumpeter, Diadem* and eight destroyers, put to sea on December 6 for the operation on the following day. The TAGs received a special briefing for this particular raid. Shown photographs of the area, their attention was drawn to a camouflaged building, thought to be an ammunition dump, which they were to strafe with their turret guns as they flew past. Stewart Crawford, one of the TAGs on the raid takes up the story.

'Having been catapulted from *Premier*, the Avengers formed up, and escorted by our Wildcat flight, led by Lt. Bill Vittle, we flew at sea-level towards the Norwegian coast. After about an hour's flying, with the coast in view, the Wildcats went ahead to strafe the gun positions, which had by now opened fire. As we entered the narrow channel, the TAGs turned their turrets on the camouflaged building, ripping it with gunfire, and smoke was seen to rise. Further up the channel, the mines having been dropped, we headed back to the carrier and just off the coast saw Bill Vittle scrambling into his dinghy. We waved to him and, as he returned our wave, little realised that we should not see him again. In the debriefing which followed, we TAGs confirmed having carried out our instructions to the letter, not realising that we had not heard the last of the matter. It was not until four months later, in April 1945, during the outward trip of a Russian Convoy, that the subject came up again. On board was a party of Norwegian servicemen, with whom we spoke of our mine-laying operations in Norway, and we were pleased to hear one express his view that the Norwegian people would always be grateful for all that the British had done. But he then went on to say that the citizens of his native Haugesund were a little upset when some British airmen shot up their local church in a raid the previous December. On some occasions, the best policy is to keep quiet and, to all of us TAGs, this was one of the occasions.'

* * * *

However, the story does not end there. In 1984, Stewart Crawford wrote to the Mayor of Haugesund and explained the circumstances of the strafing of their church, and received a most magnanimous reply, saying that they understood the need for the actions taken during the war and that they "forgave" all concerned. The Mayor went on to explain their feelings at the time with a simple yet most moving anecdote.

> 'Most of us felt like the small boy who, when told by a German soldier to go to the shelter during an air-raid, replied, "It's not us they are after."'

* * * *

A few days later, the two carriers, supported by *Devonshire* and destroyer escort, returned to the Norwegian coast for Operation LACERATE, the laying of mines in the shipping channels at Ramsoysund; six Avengers from each carrier, supported by Wildcats, participated. Attacks by enemy torpedo bombers at night were driven off and one JU88 shot down. A second operation, scheduled for the following day, had to be abandoned, owing to severe gales which damaged the flight deck of the *Premier*. Returning to Scapa, where damaged aircraft were loaded for transfer to the mainland, *Premier* then proceeded to the Clyde, tying up at the Tail-of-the-Bank, where aircrew were granted leave.

In the new year, *Premier* returned to Scapa and, on January 11, sailed with *Trumpeter, Dido* and four destroyers to join First Cruiser Squadron for Operation SPELLBINDER, the attack on an enemy convoy and mine-laying off the coast. Enemy air attacks were repulsed by the carriers' Wildcats, which shot down one plane. On the following day, in Operation GRATIS, Avengers and Wildcats of 856 and 846 Squadrons once again laid mines in Karmoysund with little enemy opposition; the task force returning to Scapa on the same day. For the next six weeks, 856 on *Premier* were engaged in a series of operations off the Norwegian coast, the first of which, a mine-lay, had to be abandoned because of heavy snow showers. In the second operation, 856's Avenger and Wildcats provided anti-submarine and fighter cover for the task force while Swordfish from *Campania* and *Nairana* carried out a night sweep of the Leads, attacking enemy shipping. Bad weather on February 4 forced the cancellation of another mine-lay but, a week later, mines were successfully laid at Skatestrommen, although one Avenger had to return with a serious oil leak, while a second failed to release its mine. Finally, on February 22, 856 Avengers, accompanied by Barracudas from *Puncher* laid mines at Haugesund yet again. No enemy aircraft scrambled from nearby Stavanger airfield but two Barracudas were shot down before releasing their mines. For the next month, 856 divided its time between RNAS Hatston and *Premier* in the Flow.

On March 19, *Premier* sailed from Scapa for Operation CUPOLA, the laying of mines in the narrow Fjord at Askvolde, accompanied by the escort carriers *Searcher* and *Queen*, the cruiser *Bellona* and destroyer escort. 853 Squadron on *Queen* was providing the anti-submarine patrols, and their Wildcats top cover for the fleet, while *Searcher*'s Wildcats would accompany 856 for the mine-laying operation. On the 20th, the weather was so rough that the take-off was delayed until the afternoon. The flight to the Norwegian coast was made at around 150 feet, to avoid radar detection, and on reaching the dropping area there was a little light flak which, having received the attention of the Wildcats, was somewhat erratic and of little hindrance. Having laid the mines, the squadron headed back to the carrier, which came into sight around 1600, her flight deck pitching to a frightening degree. Nevertheless, all Avengers eventually landed safely, although that of TAG, Stewart Crawford, had to make several attempts before doing so. He was sitting in the rear cockpit, breathing a sigh of relief, when the door was suddenly thrust open.

> 'It was an armourer who spluttered, "For Christ's sake, the bloody thing's still there!" He was obviously referring to our magnetic mine. Before we had time to recover from the shock, came the announcement over the ship's Tannoy, "Would the crew of the aircraft which has just landed report to the Captain on the bridge at once." It was with some

trepidation that we climbed up to the bridge, to be met by a stern-faced Captain Gardiner who demanded an explanation for our landing with a live mine, thereby endangering the safety of the ship and its crew. The pilot manfully admitted that it was his mistake in selecting the wrong switch which had prevented the mine being released. Normally, I would have checked whether the mine had dropped, by looking into the bomb-bay through the Perspex panel in the rear cabin but, on this occasion, the smaller type of mine carried was not visible. After a lecture upon the seriousness of our actions, first by the Captain and then the Commander Operations, we were suitably admonished and, with relief, made our way to the sanctuary of the Ready Room. Luckily, for our peace of mind, it was found that the mines dropped by the remaining aircraft had successfully blocked the channel, so the squadron's efforts had not been wasted even if our own journey had been!'

In April, 856 was faced with a new challenge when it embarked on *Premier* for what was to be the last wartime Russian convoy operation, JW/RA66; accompanying *Premier* was the escort carrier *Vindex* and the 19th Escort Group. By this stage of the war, the allied armies were over-running Europe, the end was in sight and an uneventful run could have been expected. The outward passage was just that, but sailing from Kola on April 29, for the return passage, German U-boats were waiting and the frigate *Goodall* was sunk with a heavy loss of life. Escort vessels were successful in sinking one of the U-boats. On the following day, 100 miles north of Murmansk, at 1640, one of 856's Avengers was returning from an anti-submarine patrol, still carrying its four depth-charges, when it made its landing approach. At the final stage, owing to heavy icing, the port wing dropped suddenly and, although the pilot retracted the undercarriage and tried to maintain flying speed, there was no chance of doing so. TAG, Stewart Crawford, was in Avenger 6BE at the time.

'I was in the turret when suddenly there was a tremendous

grinding of metal followed by a deathly silence. The plane was on its side and my first thought was to release the turret escape hatch and drop into the sea some 60 feet below but, after further reflection, I quickly abandoned that idea and decided to escape via the rear cabin door which was facing upwards. In my haste to extricate myself from the turret, I forgot to unplug my helmet from the intercom socket and so my exit was brought to an abrupt halt by the earphone lead around my throat. In dealing with this, I made matters worse by accidentally inflating my Mae West which made escape from the confined space of the turret even more difficult but, by this time, the engine was on fire and added to my desperation. Finally, I wrenched myself free, crawled into the cabin and opened the door, only to realise that, with the rear fuselage suspended in mid-air, I was now faced with crawling along the side of the plane to reach the flight deck. With the fire-hose jets being sprayed over the plane, I was in great danger of being knocked over the side, but eventually I reached the safety of the deck, to be met by my CO, who asked me if I had made sure that the bomb switches were on safe. Although a valid question for those having to deal with the wrecked plane, to me, whose mental processes were in a highly excitable state, it was an irrelevance which I dismissed as such; or so I was told afterwards. There was no sign of my crew members, who had escaped quicker than I and were, by then, in the Sick Bay.

'Later, when thinking of the incident, I realised that it was the first time that I had been in the turret to land on; normally I would have sat on the bench seat in the rear cabin, without strapping myself in. I have since wondered what made me change my mind on that occasion.'

As the convoy completed its passage, German resistance continued to crumble and, on May 8 at midnight, all hostilities in European waters ceased. Two days later, *Premier* reached Scapa and was the last wartime carrier to enter the Flow. 856 flew ashore to Hatston, where they remained for a few weeks but with plans for their transfer to the British Pacific Fleet being cancelled, the squadron was disbanded on June 15.

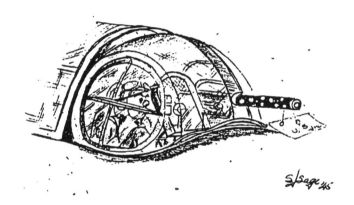

Outlook unsettled

INDIAN OCEAN

1944

The first Avenger squadron to be sent to the Indian Ocean was 851 which arrived there in March, 1944, closely followed, in April, by 832 and 845. It was only now, after their enforced inactivity over the past three months, that the squadron was able to start working up, first with the *Shah* and then ashore at RNAS Katukurunda and RNAS Colombo Racecourse. It was during this period that, on a training exercise, a crew was lost when their Avenger crashed into the sea off Ceylon. Leading Airman C. D. Airey, one of the eight members of 45A Course who had joined the squadron, was the TAG.

In May, 851 squadron rejoined *Shah* which, with *Begum,* formed an Escort Carrier Group assigned to trade protection duties, operating for the first two months from Trincomalee. The Carrier Group made sweeps in the Bay of Bengal, 851 and 832 flying anti-submarine searches on alternate days. It was during such a sweep that an Avenger from 851 ditched while attempting to land. The TAG, Bertie Beckett, was in the turret at the time and, as was so often the case when an Avenger ditched, the aircraft remained afloat allowing time for the crew to escape and to remove the dinghy from its stowage. The crew then climbed into the inflated dinghy and paddled over to their escort vessel, the frigate *Findhorn,* which picked them up. They remained on board for the next week or so until the ships put into port and they were able to rejoin *Shah*. For Bertie Beckett it was a pleasant interval as he was invited into the wardroom and, as he recalls.

'I was the envy of the officers when, at dinner, my daily tot of rum was brought to me by the steward on a silver tray!'.

But on re-boarding *Shah*, things soon reverted to normal when Bertie was sent for by the Master-at-Arms to explain why he had not reported his coming aboard to the Regulating Office.

At the end of July, the Carrier Group moved to Mombasa, West Africa, from where sweeps were made off the Seychelles and it was on the first of these that the Carrier Group sank *U-198* on August 12. The U-boat was first sighted by Avengers on the 10th and the position, where it was seen to dive, marked with smoke floats. An intensive search was made over the next two days until, on the 12th, it was located and attacked by two of the escorts, the frigate *Findhorn* and the sloop *Godaveri* (RIN). After the attack, oil and wreckage found on the surface confirmed the sinking for which action one of the TAGs of 851 was mentioned in dispatches. However, TAG, Bertie Beckett, was unable to participate in the action as he was once again aboard one of the escort vessels, having crashed on take-off for a patrol on August 10. Unlike the previous ditching, this one was much more spectacular for onlookers but not for the crew, who were lucky to survive.

'I was in the turret and as the plane drew level with the bridge, I felt it lift off but then, suddenly, the tail-end jerked violently left and right, the port wing dropped sharply and it nose-dived into the sea upside down, just ahead of the carrier's bows. Fortunately, as we were below the surface, we were blissfully unaware of the danger from the ship which, in the event, had made an emergency turn to starboard to avoid us. It was not until we were about 8 to 10 feet down that the plane filled with water and I was able to remove the turret escape-hatch to get out. In the confines of the turret, upside down, underwater, and with the plane gradually sinking, I was desperate to escape but my first attempt was prevented when the lead, connecting my helmet-earphones to the intercom socket, got caught around my neck. Having disconnected the lead, I managed, after a bit of a struggle, to free myself and shot up to the surface where I found the pilot and observer, who had escaped some seconds earlier. The dinghy had gone down with the plane and so, as the sea was extremely rough, we decided to join hands so as to avoid getting separated by the violent motion of the waves. The pilot was suffering from cuts and bruises to his face but the observer and I were uninjured. Because of the sea conditions, we could not be seen by the escort vessel searching for us although we did have a few glimpses of its masthead from time to time. After about 50 minutes, we were eventually spotted and picked up by a whaler, which had a difficult task rowing in the rough seas but at last we boarded the RIN sloop *Cauvery.* I was again invited into the wardroom and spent a pleasant few days aboard until we reached harbour. Back on the *Shah,* I remembered to report my presence to the Regulating Office thus saving myself another dressing down by the Master-at-Arms.'

Leaving *Shah* in October, 851 flew ashore to RAF Minneriya from where it operated for the next three months. While there, 851 was to lose one of its planes on a night exercise in early January. The squadron took off for a flare-dropping exercise with the TAG, Larry Larwood, aboard one of the planes. He had been with 851 from the start and expected to remain with it for some time longer subject, of course, to any unforeseen events, and wartime flying was not unknown for such. The planes, having reached the target area, were deploying for the exercise with Larry, seated in the rear cabin of his Avenger, adjusting his radio;

'The next moment, or so it seemed to me, I found myself in the sea, it was pitch black and as I struggled to keep afloat, wondering what had happened, I heard shouting nearby. I recognised my pilot's voice and shouted back, whereupon he swam over to my side. There was no sign or sound of the observer and as our eyes had now adjusted to the darkness, we could make out the outline of the shore. We started swimming but I realised at once, from the intense pain in my legs, that I must have sustained some injuries, nevertheless, we had to reach the shore so together we headed that way. I was thankful for the buoyancy of my Mae West and the help of my pilot, who had survived uninjured. After a time, we heard voices and then caught sight of lanterns in the distance; it was a canoe with outrigger used by local fishermen. Our shouts attracted their attention and they quickly paddled towards us and picked us up. As the fishermen skilfully rode the breakers to get us ashore, we realised that, as swimmers, we would never have survived the savage undertow of the breakers. I was lifted from the boat and carried ashore where the fishermen lit a bonfire which not only gave light and warmth but also acted as a beacon for rescuers. In the meantime, the pilot, with one of the fishermen as a guide, went to get help and I eventually found myself in Colombo Naval Hospital. Soon after, *Shah,* with 851 aboard, sailed for South Africa for a refit, but for me the war was over!'

Larry spent four to five months in hospital, having sustained dislocated and broken ankles and miscellaneous lacerations; when he returned to the UK, the war in Europe had finished.

Later, it was revealed that the accident was caused by the pilot being temporarily blinded by a flare dropped from another aircraft; as a result he had dived into the sea. The Avenger must have broken up on impact, thus allowing the unconscious TAG to float to the surface where he luckily revived. The body of the observer was washed ashore several days after the accident.

* * * *

For 845 squadron personnel, and 832 who were also aboard, the passage through the Mediterranean was uneventful, though two weeks of enforced idleness with endless games of Monopoly, cinema shows and other pastimes became very tiresome, so much so that I actually looked forward to my duties, organising lookouts for the gun crews. At Port Said, the squadron transferred to SS *Aronda*, a coal-burning ship of around 4,500 tons, lacking the facilities of the *Strathnaver*, as we were to find out very quickly. On the second day aboard, 50 or so of us POs put in a complaint about sharing a mess with ratings of lower rank and, as a result, were moved to our own mess; just as awful but slightly less crowded. As we progressed south through the Suez Canal and then down the Red Sea, it became warmer and by the time we reached Aden, where the ship put in for five days, the weather was distinctly hot. We were now issued with two sets of khaki cotton shirt and shorts, with very little regard for fit, but anything was better than the blue serge uniform in that heat. On March 28, we set out on the last leg of our voyage, reaching Colombo on April 4, by which time most of us were suffering from prickly heat rash. What a relief to get ashore after five weeks of cramped conditions and with nothing to do but grouse. We left Colombo by train for a two-hour journey to RNAS Katukurunda about 35 miles south.

It took a little time to adapt to the climate, fauna, and flora, and to living in thatched huts with no windows or doors, but, by April 10, the regular squadron routines were established and the squadron had received its new Avengers. The first week was spent on testing the new equipment and resolving any problems which arose, then, the usual flying exercises began again. However, there was an indication of things to come when the squadron carried out simulated bombing attacks on *Illustrious* and, subsequently, USS *Saratoga*. On April 26, the packing of squadron stores and personal kit commenced and early on the 29th we boarded a convoy of lorries for Colombo where we embarked on the *Illustrious*. She was a fleet carrier of some distinction and far removed from the escort carrier *Chaser* upon which the squadron had previously served. The TAGs' mess, shared with the 832 TAGs, was just below the flight deck on the starboard bow and so had portholes, which could be opened in the daytime, and were of benefit in the tropics. However, the ship had the traditional RN messing arrangements which meant having all food collected by messmen from central galleys for eating on the messdeck which was also the place where, at night, hammocks were slung. The first night aboard was, as I expressed it at the time, "horrible night, hot sweating and itching;" no wonder the next night was spent on the flight deck! One disadvantage of the location of the TAG mess was the distance away of the washrooms, located some decks down in the bowels of the ship. I still recall the physical discomfort of the morning visit for the customary wash and shave when a few hundred others were also doing the same thing. At sea, the water-tight hatches would be in place so that to move from deck to deck, it was necessary to scramble through the access covers, hinged metal plates similar to a manhole cover. As you descended, it became hotter and more humid so that you were sweating profusely on joining the queue for the washroom. Toilet complete and feeling a little fresher, you then faced the climb back up, with the inevitable delays at each deck level, very conscious of the fact that, in scrambling through the hatches, you were wiping the grime left by hundreds of feet, yours included, from the access covers to your hands and clothes. On reaching the mess, you found that you were hotter and dirtier than before you started; obviously, work study was not a factor which entered into the design of ships in those days!

For the next week, the *Illustrious* remained in Colombo harbour and shore leave was granted on most days; it was during this time that, I recall, one of the TAGs asking our Chief, Tom Woolmer, whether the rumour going around of a strike on a place called Surabaya was correct. He was obviously astonished at the question and refused to answer, thereby, in a way, confirming the truth of the rumour; security, it seemed, was a little lax. On May 3rd, *Illustrious* put to sea for the day to allow the resident Barracuda squadrons to fly ashore and the Avengers of 845 and 832 to fly aboard. Having flown off, the Barracudas formed up prior to flying past the ship at low level but, as I watched, one Barracuda hit the tail of another, its airscrew smashing the rudder and elevators, causing the second aircraft to spin into the sea, a few hundred feet below. The crew of this Barracuda, the pilot and two ground staff, were killed but the other managed to land in the sea and the crew was rescued. After this tragedy, two Corsairs crashed on landing but there were no casualties; the Corsair fighter gave an impression of sheer brute strength with its inverted gull wing, enormous Double Wasp engine and large Hamilton propeller but, with its poor landing characteristics, it always brought an overriding air of tension to the flight deck when it was landing on.

Finally, at 1700 on Saturday, May 6, *Illustrious* and USS *Saratoga* put to sea, meeting up with the rest of the fleet some miles off the coast. It was an impressive sight, the two carriers, battleships *Queen Elizabeth, Valiant,* and *Richelieu,* battlecruiser *Renown,* five cruisers, and fourteen destroyers. The USS *Saratoga* was by far the largest ship in the fleet, twice the tonnage of *Illustrious* with a 900 feet flight deck and a great slab-sided funnel which made her unmistakable. Furthermore, she had come direct from the Pacific where she had taken part in the great carrier battles of the Eastern Solomons, and the amphibious actions in the Gilbert and Marshall Islands where Japanese forces had been smashed. In March, she had come to help the Eastern Fleet to attack Japanese bases in the Indian Ocean, starting with an attack on Sabang in April and now the big one on Surabaya before returning to the Pacific Fleet; it was a very reassuring thought to know that she was with the Fleet. But there had been previous co-operation with the Royal Navy in early 1943, when *Victorious* had been loaned to the US Navy for service in the Pacific, during which time not only did the two ships serve together but 832 squadron had actually served aboard USS *Saratoga* for a month of that time.

Anti-submarine patrols by Avengers were started immediately, covering an area up to 120 miles ahead of the Fleet. The weather was squally at times and it became progressively hotter as we steamed south, crossing the equator at 1130 on May 9, when the customary ceremony of 'crossing the line' was dispensed with owing to more pressing matters. On that day there was firing practice by a number of the ships' guns crews and, in the afternoon, the first practice strike, with 20 Avengers and 16 Corsairs attacking the Fleet. Aircrews started having their first briefings for the raid on Surabaya, one of which was devoted to the make-up of the Japanese Fleet, which intelligence reports indicated was based at Singapore, comprising 5 battleships, 3 carriers together with a cruiser force. In March, three Japanese cruisers had made a foray into the Indian Ocean, sinking two merchant ships, and there was the possibility that their fleet could be provoked into action by our presence. The weather was now becoming cooler, as we progressed further south, which was a relief from the sticky conditions of the tropics. On May 12, 100 aircraft took part in the second strike exercise on the Fleet, lasting for almost three and half hours. During the flight, I had the first nagging pain of toothache and decided that a visit to the dentist was called for. There was a first-rate dentist's surgery on *Illustrious* and the offending molar was removed, to my great relief; it has since struck me as rather bizarre to have had a course of dental treatment, I had a number of fillings later, at such a time and place.

On May 15, the Fleet anchored in Exmouth Gulf, on the east coast of Australia, some 1000 miles south of our target Surabaya. There, ships were refuelled, by the tankers stationed in the Gulf for the purpose, and by 1730 on the same day the Fleet had set sail northwards.

May 16, the day before the raid, was taken up with more briefings and preparations for the morrow. On the subject of aircraft recognition, it was generally agreed that the best policy would be to fire at any aircraft other than Avengers, Hellcats, Corsairs and Dauntlesses, which we could all recognise; it certainly simplified things. After the briefings, we were issued with jungle suits, emergency rations, maps, Javanese currency and 0.38 Colt revolvers. Then it was time to climb into the hammock and wait for an early call to action. We were called at 0500 and, after a quick visit to the washroom and then some light refreshments in the mess, we made our way to the TAG ready-room to get kitted-up and await for the call to 'man aircraft'. All the aircraft were ranged on the flight deck in order of take-off, Corsairs first, 832 Avengers next and 845 Avengers last, so that, when the call came, it took quite some minutes to thread your way through the tightly-packed aircraft and get aboard. Being among the last in the queue, we had to wait some minutes before our turn came for take-off but finally we went thundering down the deck and were away.

One of our aircraft ditched on take-off and so the squadron was one aircraft short as we formed up and set course as part of the second wave of bombers. My aircraft was flying in the starboard end position of the second V formation and, as I sat in the turret, I felt a little anxious, knowing that it would be the obvious target for enemy fighters. The formations climbed steadily to 12,000 feet and, looking down, as we approached the coast, my attention was drawn to a warship which was in the process of executing an 180 degree turn, probably thinking that it would be safer in port than out at sea. It was the foaming white circle of the ship's wake which had revealed its presence so vividly; luckily for its crew, they were safe from attack, as our targets were some 100 miles further on, Crossing Java, the terrain was mountainous with a number of volcanic craters, some gently-smoking, not an ideal place for a forced landing, I thought. Still no sign of enemy fighters as we prepared to dive, but, as we did so, a pillar of black smoke started rising from the Wonokromo oil refinery, the target of the US Dauntlesses in the first wave. The 845 target was the Braat naval engineering works, a complex of large concrete buildings with a POW camp across the road from it. We had been warned of the serious consequences of any inaccuracy in our bombing, so the dropping height was set at around 2000 feet to reduce the possibility of any bombs going astray. Having released our 4 x 500 1b bombs, we pulled out, and I recall flying over the roof of a huge building as we raced to the assembly area a few miles distant. As we roared along at a few hundred feet, I remember seeing native fishermen in their dugout canoes and it struck me as incongruous to see the peaceful occupation of fishing amidst the death and destruction which was going on all around. At the rendezvous position, we joined other circling bombers adopting a somewhat amorphous formation, and, after a couple of circuits, set off on the return flight. There was no time to re-group in squadrons and, to my relief, my pilot had taken up a position in the middle of a mixed group of Avengers and Dauntlesses. Flying back over Java, I noticed light flak coming up in our direction and subsequently discovered that, in error, we were being led over a Japanese airfield. The accompanying fighters could not resist such a target and dived to strafe the field, leaving the bombers to look after themselves. Fortunately, the enemy were taken by surprise and we returned to the Fleet unmolested after being in the air for three and a half hours.

George Smith, who trained with me as a TAG, was serving with 832 squadron and recalls his memories of the raid.

'I remember being awakened at a very early hour and, after briefing and other preliminaries, taking off at 0635. After forming up with the rest of the squadron, we spent some time circling the Fleet, to allow the other squadrons to take off and get into position, before setting course for Java. There was a clear blue sky, and as the formations sped towards the enemy coast everything seemed surprisingly peaceful up at 12,000 ft. Just before reaching the coast, I cocked my 0.5 Browning, never an easy task in the confines of the turret, and fired a test burst. The flight over Java was uneventful and as we approached the target we commenced the dive. The task of 832 Squadron was to bomb the naval installations in the harbour area, and after releasing our four 500lb bombs, we flew low alongside the jetties. As we swept along, I swung the turret towards the buildings, and spotting a group of uniformed men running for shelter, I gave them a burst to help them on their way. There was a great deal of billowing black smoke from the oil storage tanks attacked by the US Dauntless dive-bombers. As we flew to the assembly area, I recall seeing below me, in the outer harbour, a rubber dinghy with a motorboat heading rapidly towards it - the dinghy was later identified as belonging to a US Dauntless shot down by anti-aircraft fire.

'The return flight was uneventful and we landed back on *Illustrious* around 1000. After debriefing, we adjourned to the mess deck for a special turkey breakfast. At the time, my thoughts regarding the operation were twofold. Firstly, satisfaction in participating in a major strike against the Japanese and, secondly, a feeling of profound relief at the absence of enemy fighters, as we had been warned to expect interception. It had been a day to remember.'

The raid, by 45 Avengers and Dauntlesses escorted by 40 Corsairs and Hellcats, was the largest carried out by the FAA at that stage of the war. Heavy damage had been caused to the oil refinery, engineering works, harbour installations and shipping, while the fighters had strafed Malang Airfield, inflicting damage on hangars, barracks and aircraft on the ground. Only one aircraft, a Dauntless, had been shot down and the crew lost. A message of congratulations was sent by Mr. Churchill to C-in-C., Eastern Fleet, Admiral Somerville, on the success of the raid. But now it was all over and we were sailing once again for Exmouth Gulf to refuel before heading back to Colombo. It was a bit of an anti-climax and I felt rather depressed after all the excitement of the previous days, accentuated by the departure of the USS *Saratoga* on the next day when, with her destroyers, she steamed past all the ships in the Fleet formed in column stretching to the horizon. She was cheered the whole length of the column and so departed to continue the war at Iwo Jima, thence to Tokyo and, finally, to the bottom of Bikini Lagoon, sunk in the atom bomb experiment of July, 1946.

The Fleet arrived at Exmouth Gulf the next day where the crew of the 845 Avenger which crashed on take-off on the day of the raid, was transferred, from the destroyer which rescued them, to *Illustrious*. The TAG concerned was Gus Furmage, who gave the rest of us a Javanese coin as a souvenir; we had to return our currency after the raid, but he had 'lost' his when he ditched - I still have it. On the return passage, the usual anti-submarine patrols were flown but otherwise it was a quiet time and I continued with my dental treatment, having three further appointments for fillings. Then, on May 27, after three weeks at sea, during which time we had covered over 7000 miles, we flew ashore to RNAS Katukurunda.

The squadron settled in again at Katukurunda for a few days before being sent on leave to Diyatalawa rest camp, located 4500 feet up in the hills, and run by the Army. It was less humid than on the coast and was pleasant enough for a short stay, though the food was poor, which we, as naval types, attributed to the army catering. It also gave, those so inclined, the opportunity to get drunk, and our RPO lost his false teeth, during his return to the mess after a heavy drinking session in the canteen - the next morning's search for the missing teeth providing great amusement for the squadron's personnel. After a week, the squadron returned to Katukurunda where little flying was done and 'make and mend', the Navy's term for an afternoon off, was granted most days. It was at this time, I put in my first CO's request for recommendation for a pilot's course. The regulations covering applications from the ranks had been considerably eased in 1943 and, having discussed the matter with my own pilot, who supported the idea, I decided to apply. Unfortunately for me, my pilot was away for the next few weeks, when my request to see the CO was granted, and so he was not there to support my application; the outcome was a qualified, "Yes - but not yet." I was disappointed but remained undeterred. In the meantime, the squadron had received orders to join *Ameer*, a newly-commissioned escort carrier of the Ruler class of 11,420 tons displacement; as with 832, we had been relegated to trade protection duties. On June 23, we embarked, putting to sea a few days later when the aircraft flew aboard and the ship sailed for Trincomalee. Then started a period of working up in the straits between Ceylon and India, the ship anchoring in the shallows at night when films were sometimes shown in the hangar. During this time, an unfortunate accident occurred during a routine maintenance check of an Avenger's turret gun while in the hangar. The armourer was testing the firing mechanism, the barrel of the gun being raised for the purpose, when a round was discharged. The bullet hit a steel girder on the deckhead and was deflected downwards, hitting a squadron rating then, ricocheting off the steel hangar deck, struck a second rating before coming to rest in an aircraft. The first rating was killed instantly, while the second was wounded in the thigh; such was the power of the 0.5 Browning gun. It saddened us to think that a life had been snatched away in such an indiscriminate fashion.

    Ameer returned to Trincomalee on July 10 and for the next four weeks remained there, awaiting suitable escorts before commencing operations. It was a frustrating time, with little to do except that which, as TAGs, we would have preferred not to do: watches with the ship's Telegraphists on communications exercises with the ships in harbour. As TAGs, we were no match for the trained Telegraphists in morse transmitting and receiving, especially as, in Avengers, morse was very rarely used, so our skill deteriorated from lack of practice and I, for one, found myself floundering badly in the exercises. Our Chief, Tom Woolmer, left the squadron around this time and we missed his authority to back us up in such matters. PO(A) Nobby Clark was the new Senior TAG but he, too, was to leave in a few months time. At last, *Ameer* put to sea, bound for Colombo, and flying started again. We reached port on August 8 and thought that operations would now begin in earnest, but things did not work out that way. After a day at sea on August 16, when a flight of Wildcats flew aboard to join the squadron, we were told that repairs to the ship's engines were needed so the squadron would go ashore for a period. There was further delay while the problem of getting the squadron ashore, as the ship was unable to put to sea, was resolved. Morale on the squadron was not improved by the news and two minor incidents with higher naval authorities did nothing to raise it. One day, an Admiral came aboard and addressed the ship's company about their future role in the Fleet and mentioned that we should not be abroad for more than another one and a half years. It was not the kind of message to raise ones spirits! The second incident also involved an Admiral, when our liberty boat, failing to salute a passing Admiral's barge, was stopped and the senior officer on board was made to accompany the Admiral, presumably for a reprimand. Such incidents are trivial in themselves but, in the circumstances of the time, they do cause resentment out of all proportion to their importance.

On August 24, it was decided to risk boosting the Avengers on the steam catapult with the ship still in harbour. It was not something which would normally be attempted, especially as it was doubtful that the ship's damaged engines could supply the maximum steam pressure required. In the event, six Avengers were successfully boosted and flew to Katukurunda where they were joined by half the squadron complement while the rest, including myself, remained aboard to do precisely nothing for two weeks then we joined the rest of the squadron at Katukurunda. My pilot had now returned and we started flying again; what a relief to get airborne even if it was back to the familiar bombing exercises. At the end of September, the squadron went on leave to Diyatalawa rest camp again but, on this occasion, I and two other TAGs, John Munro and Fred Townsend, were fortunate in finding a delightful refuge for our stay and, in fact, for other occasions in the future. It happened quite accidentally when we, all three, hired bicycles to ride the 22 miles to the town of Badulla, which was some 2000 feet lower down. This meant that the ride was all downhill and the return journey was achieved by travelling on the train, with the bikes in the luggage van. While in Badulla, we happened to visit a planters' club which RAF personnel were authorised to use for leave. On meeting the lady who organised the scheme, wife of a tea-planter at a nearby estate, we arranged to go there to stay instead of the rest camp. After a meal, we returned to Diyatalawa and, on the next day, returned with our luggage to the UVA Goose Club, as it was known. As a planters' club, it was well-equipped with tennis courts, billiard tables, bar and fine dining-room with meals to match. As naval types, we were not allowed to use the RAF dormitories, even if we had wished to do, but had our own private accommodation in the Masonic Hall which was specially arranged for us.

On return from leave, the squadron received orders to go aboard *Ameer* again, but these were cancelled a few hours later and so flying began again. However, the weather turned extremely wet and the flying programme was badly affected; the highest rainfall on one day was 7.08 inches.

For some time, there had been rumours circulating on the squadron that some crews might be leaving, but I had tended to ignore them as just gossip. Imagine my utter surprise when I was told by my pilot that three crews were going to join 849 Squadron and that his was one of them. However, the TAGs of these crews would not be going, instead, three of the less experienced TAGs would be drafted, but not as members of those crews. I was most unhappy at the prospect of losing the pilot and observer with whom I had been flying for the past 21 months, but it appeared that there was no alternative. They left the squadron on October 20 and, on the same day, we moved to RNAS Colombo Racecourse where, messing accommodation being full, ratings were to live on the terraces of the old grandstand. Needless to say, the following morning our CO was inundated with complaints about the filthy conditions, and he arranged with the *Ameer* that we should live aboard and travel to the airfield each day by bus. The arrangement suited us fine, as when flying finished, we were at liberty to go into Colombo to spend our free time and then catch a boat back to the ship to sleep. Around this time, the number of aircraft on the squadron was reduced to eight, so the loss of the three crews brought numbers into balance. I had not been allocated to a particular crew so, with the absence of the Senior TAG, I flew with the CO for a couple of weeks. Soon after, Nobby Clark was drafted to the UK and John Munro was appointed as Senior TAG in his place. On November 10, returning early to *Ameer,* I was surprised to meet my old pilot aboard; we exchanged news and he mentioned his new PO TAG on 849; it proved to be the last time that I should see him.

A week later, the CO broke the news that the squadron was to move to an RAF camp located in a remote area north of Trincomalee. As the *Ameer* was due to go into dry-dock, the remaining Avengers aboard had to be catapulted off beforehand; it happened to be my first such take-off. The journey to our destination, Vavuniya, 180 miles from Colombo, started at 1700 and finished at 1730; our convoy consisting of 17 lorries and 15 cwt trucks. The camp was certainly different, situated in the middle of what had been jungle, the undergrowth having been cleared but the trees left. Rough roads had been laid down, each named after a London street, for example, Harley Street where the medical section was housed. The buildings were the usual thatched roof huts with window opening fitted with flaps to lower at night. It was situated in an area where malaria was rife and so strict precautions were enforced to prevent its spread; in addition to the use of customary mosquito nets at night, all sleeping quarters were sprayed regularly. No doubt due to the surrounding trees, the place was very damp and clothes soon became mildewed, particularly our blue uniforms, which were packed away. The remedy of placing them out to dry off also had its disadvantages as the buttons disappeared as the result of marauding tree rats. The airfield was just a clearing in the jungle and was the base for two RAF fighter squadrons. There was no apparent purpose in 845 Squadron being there and only a few miscellaneous flights were made. Aircrew were granted leave and the eight TAGs travelled by lorry, equipped with armchairs in the back, to the rest camp, except for the three of us who went to the Uva Goose Club. The journey was memorable as the driver of the lorry had been a 'wall-of-death' driver at some time in his civilian career and was keen to show us! We hit a car at one point and the Singhalese driver was naturally far from pleased but, after exchanging particulars, we continued on our way - no doubt the Navy received the bill for damages. We returned to Vavuniya ten days later only to find that the squadron was on the move again. On Christmas eve, we travelled to Trincomalee where *Ameer*, engines repaired, was awaiting us. Christmas aboard was quite enjoyable but, on Boxing day, we discovered that we should be leaving in a few days time.

* * * *

Disembarking from the *Aronda* on April 5, 832 Squadron went to RNAS Katukurunda and, after a period of working up, embarked on *Illustrious* for the raid on Surabaya, with 845, as described elsewhere. On disembarking, the squadron then joined the escort carrier *Begum*, which was to be its base for trade protection operations until the end of the year. It is hard to understand the reasoning behind the decision to relegate an experienced squadron like 832 to trade protection while, at the same time, sending out newly-formed squadrons for the British Pacific Fleet but, from a TAG's viewpoint generally, some squadron moves could appear hard to justify.

Begum, together with *Shah* with 851 on board, formed an escort carrier group which, from their base at Trincomalee, made sweeps in the Bay of Bengal, searching for enemy submarines and shipping. On the sweeps, the Avengers were sent out daily to fly specific sectors of the search area so covering a segment of the ocean, many thousand square miles in extent. As with most CVE trade protection activities, their success was mainly of a negative nature, in that enemy submarines were deterred from attacking and so fewer ships were sunk. In the middle of July, crews were sent on leave to a Rest Camp at RAF Minneriya, situated in the hills south of Trincomalee.

On returning from leave, the squadron found that the *Begum*, together with the rest of the Carrier Group, was moving to a fresh base, namely Mombasa, on the west coast of Africa. Here, the Group remained for two months, making hunter/killer sweeps off the Seychelles and it was on the first of these that *U-198* was sunk, on August 12, as described elsewhere. No further successes were achieved in the following months and, after a rest period at RAF Port Reitz, the Carrier Group returned to Ceylon in early October. Shortly before reaching port, George Smith, who had served as a TAG on 832 since it had re-equipped with Avengers in December, 1942, suffered another attack of Dengue fever and, after ten days in hospital, was drafted to 756 Squadron as a Gunnery Instructor. Following a short stay at RNAS Katukurunda, 832 rejoined *Begum* for further operations, mainly in the Bay of Bengal. However, 851 went ashore to RAF Minneriya, operating from there for the next three months.

Around this time, TAG, George Rock, joined 832 on the *Begum*, having previously been with 756 Squadron at RNAS Katukurunda. George recalls that the patrols were flown at dawn and dusk, with usually six aircraft taking part, each armed with four depth charges. The aircraft would fan out until about twenty miles apart, thus sweeping a swathe a hundred miles wide, It was fairly tedious work, keeping a sharp lookout for a periscope looking like a feather on the ocean surface below. The return to the carrier presented no problem, but on the odd occasion, when visibility was poor, locating its exact position might necessitate making a square search in the estimated vicinity. On one occasion the weather was so bad that all other aircrafts returned early, whereas George's crew pressed on and completed the patrol only to be signalled, by Aldis lamp, as they approached one of the escort vessels, 'Doctor Livingstone, I presume.' It was on one such dawn patrol, before first light, that a catapult failure caused an Avenger to ditch with TAG, Joe Hughes, aboard. The crew managed to escape and, as the carrier turned full circle around them, they could be heard shouting by those on deck. After dropping flame floats to indicate their position, the *Begum* sailed on, leaving the attendant destroyer to effect the rescue; the crew rejoining the ship two days later by means of breeches-buoy.

Occasionally, the *Begum* called in at Vishakhapatnam, a small port on the north-east coast of India. The harbour was small, with a narrow entrance flanked by hills on both sides. The first time that the ship approached the harbour entrance, where local sightseers had gathered on the nearby hills to watch the event, those of the ship's company lined up on deck, for the ceremony of entering harbour, started to lose their balance. As the result of an optical illusion, it appeared to them that the hills were moving, not the ship, and so, in not adjusting their stance for the motion of the ship, they lost their balance. After that, the ceremony was observed while standing at ease instead of at attention.

Towards the end of December, the *Begum* put into Colombo for repairs to the catapult, and 832 flew ashore to the RNAS, where it continued with the anti-submarine sweeps. But the squadron was nearing the end of its operational days and, in the middle of January, leaving behind its aircraft and ground crews, the aircrews rejoined *Begum* for passage home to the UK. The squadron's last operational action was accompanied by a most unusual event, the boosting of the ship's piano! There were still two Avengers aboard and it was only prudent that the repaired catapult should be tested before committing them to its use. The first test was the piano, mounted on a sledge, which was successfully launched, making a whining noise as it sailed through the air, before smashing to pieces on impact with the sea. The next two tests were made with two Barracuda aircraft, stripped of all equipment and engines but filled with ballast to increase the weight. All tests being satisfactory, the two remaining Avengers were launched, with crews from 845 Squadron to fly them ashore. When the *Begum* reached the UK, on February 21, 832 Squadron was disbanded.

OPERATION OUTFLANK

During the last quarter of 1944, four Avenger squadrons, which were to join the British Pacific Fleet, arrived in Ceylon. Three of these, 849, 854 and 857, had taken passage in the escort carriers, *Activity* and *Rajah*, calling in at RN Maintenance Yards in southern India for re-equipping, before continuing to RNAS Katukurunda, in Ceylon, for working up. There, they were joined by 820 Squadron having flown ashore from *Indefatigable* in early December. Before going to the Pacific, the squadrons were to be deployed against enemy targets in the Indian Ocean, on their respective carriers, *Victorious, Illustrious, Indomitable and Indefatigable.*

The Sumatran oilfields provided Japan with a large proportion of its aviation spirit and, for this reason, a series of operations to destroy them was planned under the code name OUTFLANK. The first of these, Operation ROBSON, was to be a raid on the oil wells and refinery at Pangkalan Brandan in north-east Sumatra. The secondary target was to be Belawan Deli, some 50 miles to the south-east, a port where tankers were supplied by a pipe-line from the oil refinery.

On December 17, Force 67, commanded by Admiral Vian and comprising the carriers *Illustrious* and *Indomitable*, three cruisers and five destroyers, sailed from Trincomalee. The weather on the 20th was inclement with poor visibility and rain squalls, but, after a short delay, the strike force was launched; 16 Avengers of 854 from *Illustrious*, 12 Avengers of 857 from *Indomitable*, 16 Hellcats, and 16 Corsairs. The Avengers each carried four 500 lb. bombs and four Corsairs were also armed with two 500 lb. each. At 0715, the striking-force departed, less one Avenger of 857 which had crashed on take-off. The weather did not improve and, as the target was enveloped in low cloud, the strike-leader, Lt/Cdr. Stuart of 857, decided to divert to the secondary target at Belawan Deli. The cloud still persisted here and the Avengers had difficulty in locating their targets but succeeded in bombing the jetty while the fighters strafed the area. There was no opposition from enemy fighters, although Hellcats shot down an enemy bomber which had strayed into their path, and the anti-aircraft fire was ineffective. The forming-up after the attack proved to be a chaotic affair partly due to the weather conditions but also to the lack of radio discipline by the fighter pilots which prevented the strike-leader from making his instructions heard. Bill Pirie, his TAG, observed,

> 'TAGs always observed radio silence except in emergencies, but the fighter bods caused havoc, their unrestrained messages blotting out all signals.'

Finally, the confusion was resolved and all aircraft returned safely and had landed on by 1050. As Force 67 sailed westward, a fighter strike was made on the airfields around Sabang but no fighter opposition was encountered. The Fleet arrived back at Trincomalee on the 22nd.

Preparations for a second attempt at Pangkalan Brandan had begun as soon as the fleet returned to port and, on January 1, Force 65, with Admiral Vian in command, put to sea for Operation LENTIL. On this occasion, the force included three fleet carriers, *Indefatigable, Victorious* and *Indomitable*, four cruisers, and eight destroyers. The two Avenger squadrons participating in the raid were 857 on *Indomitable* and 849 on *Victorious*, each carrier also carried a complement of fighter aircraft being Hellcats and Corsairs respectively, while *Indefatigable* carried Seafires, Fireflies and photo-reconnaissance Hellcats.

As the enemy had been alerted by the last raid, it was decided to alter the flying-off position to avoid sending the fleet into the Malacca Strait as previously. The strike force would now be flown off from a position between Simalur Island and the west coast of Sumatra entailing a flight of 80 miles overland starting with the Wilhelmina range of mountains rising to 10,000 feet. The plan was to approach the coast at low level, to avoid detection, then climb to 12,000 feet, cross the peaks, and descend to 10,000 feet, using the descent to increase speed.

On January 4, Force 65 reached the flying-off position and, around 0600, the fighter Ramrods, of Hellcats and Corsairs, were launched to strafe the airfields around the target area; the Avengers and escort flying off around 0730. After reaching the coast, the ascent began and as the heavily-loaded Avengers struggled to gain height one of them, from 849 Squadron, had engine failure and dropped out of formation with smoke streaming from its engine. There was no sign of enemy fighters but as the strike force approached the target they were met by heavy anti-aircraft fire. As the Avengers deployed to attack, a group of Oscars suddenly approached and were immediately engaged by the fighter escort. Five Oscars were shot down during the ensuing dog-fights but, in the meantime, the Avengers were left unprotected while making their bombing runs. Despite some light flak, the Avengers pressed home their attacks and, although hampered by smoke from burning fuel tanks, considerable damage to the refinery was inflicted. On their way to the rendezvous, the Avengers had few fighters as escort but, luckily, no enemy aircraft were encountered, either then, or on the return to the fleet. All aircraft landed safely apart from a Firefly which ran out of fuel and ditched near the *Indefatigable*. The Avenger lost by 849 managed to reach the sea and, having jettisoned its bombs, ditched safely some five miles from the shore. The crew took to their dinghy and, having attracted the attention of fighters sent to look for them, were rescued, after three anxious hours, by *Undine,* one of two destroyers sent to pick them up. The pilot, Lt.(A) D. Judd, had previously served on 845 Squadron as Senior Pilot; his TAG at the time was PO(A) R. Murphy.

Force 65 returned to Trincomalee on January 7 after a successful strike. The results had been good; apart from the damage to the refinery from the Avengers' bombs, the Ramrod had destroyed seven aircraft on the ground and two in the air, while the Fireflies had each launched their eight 60 lb. rockets at targets in the town near the refinery. In addition, the escorts had, of course, shot down five Oscars without loss although, in their enthusiasm for combat, they had neglected their duties in respect of the Avengers. This shortcoming was caused, to some extent, by radio failure which forced the escort leader and two others to return to the fleet, thus impairing the co-ordination of the escort function.

Preparations for the creation of the British Pacific Fleet had been going on for many months and their culmination was the assembling, at Trincomalee, of Force 63, commanded by Admiral Vian, which included the 1st Aircraft Carrier Squadron made up of *Illustrious, Indefatigable, Indomitable* and *Victorious*, together with the battleship *King George V,* four cruisers and ten destroyers; the second battleship, *Howe,* had, by then sailed for Australia direct. The plan was to complete the third phase of Operation OUTFLANK, code-named MERIDIAN, while sailing to, what was to be, the British Pacific Fleet's home base at Sydney, Australia. The target was to be the refineries near Palembang, a town in south Sumatra, forty miles from the east coast. The town was situated on the north bank of the Musi river, a few miles upstream of the confluence with the river Komerine. There were two refineries, Pladjoe and Soengei Gerong, which were located either side of the Komerine river at its confluence. They had been in Japanese possession since 1942, and although partly destroyed before being abandoned, were, in January 1945, in full production and capable of handling 3 million tons of crude oil each year, an amount which the Japanese could ill-afford to lose. Because of their importance, the refineries were strongly defended by heavy and light anti-aircraft batteries and, unknown to the fleet, a barrage of balloons around the perimeter. Furthermore, there was a number of fighter squadron bases, within the surrounding area, which could prove a serious threat to the Avengers when making the 300 mile round trip across Sumatra from their launch point off the west coast. It was considered that there would need to be three strikes to complete the destruction of the refineries while a subsidiary raid would be made on Mana, on the west coast, where a bomber-reconnaissance squadron was based. It was planned to bomb the runway in order to neutralise the threat posed by the squadron's presence so near to the fleet.

Prior to the fleet's departure, a full-scale rehearsal was undertaken on January 13 with a practice strike on Colombo in the morning and fighter sweeps off Trincomalee later in the day. An Avenger of 820 Squadron crashed during the former exercise and the TAG, PO(A) L.E. Cole, was killed - a sad beginning for the squadron. Force 63 sailed on January 16 with the greatest number of aircraft ever assembled by the FAA up to that time, 238 in total, of which 75 were Avengers. For briefing on the strike, a scale model of the refineries had been built showing every detail of the specific targets to be attacked. The assistance of former members of the refineries staff had enabled those units of the plant which it was essential to destroy to be identified and their locations accurately located on the model. Each squadron was given its own targets which, in turn, were allotted to individual crews so the model was subject to much study over the days leading up to the flying off position, originally planned for January 22. In the event, bad weather prevented the launch on both the 22nd and 23rd, so it was not until the 24th that the rain squalls had dispersed, although the cloud base was still low when the order for the launch was made at 0615. For MERIDIAN 1, the attack on the Pladjoe refinery, the strike force was 47 Avengers, armed with 4 x 500 lb. bombs each, escorted by 60 fighters with a further 24 fighters making Ramrod sweeps of the airfields. The force for the subsidiary raid on Mana consisted of 5 Avengers and 4 fighters, making 140 aircraft in total. In the event, only 40 Avengers reached the target, two being damaged in a deck accident on *Indefatigable*, while on *Victorious* one failed to start and four returned prematurely. On take-off, owing to the low cloud base, the strike force had some difficulties forming up but departed soon after 0700. It crossed the coast at 4,500 feet, by which time the weather was fine and clear, and climbed to over 12,000 feet to cross the Barisan mountain range. Fifteen miles from the target, the first cry of "Bandits" was heard over the radio after which a dozen or so enemy fighters dived steeply out of the sun and succeeded, in some cases, in penetrating the fighter cover to attack the Avengers. However, the attackers themselves were soon caught up in the wild confusion of dog-fights in which a large proportion of the Corsairs and Hellcats were engaged thus leaving the bombers with fewer escorts than was planned. At their approach, the heavy AA batteries around the refineries opened fire and, to their consternation and alarm, the crews could see barrage balloons ascending on all sides of the target. There had been no consideration of balloons in their briefing and so their sudden appearance was unsettling to the pilots who were just preparing to attack. No. 1 Bomber Wing, 857 and 849, dived first, releasing their bombs around 3000 feet, and immediately made for the rendezvous. No. 2 Wing, 854 and 820, followed with their attack but found that billowing smoke from damaged oil tanks forced some crews to switch to alternative targets. As the individual Avengers headed for the rendezvous, encountering heavy anti-aircraft fire, they were again particularly vulnerable to attack by enemy fighters despite the patrolling Fireflies and those escort fighters which still remained with them and, in the event, a number of them were attacked. 849 TAG,

Harry Copping, suddenly found a Jap on his tail.

'It was close behind but, being unable to fire the turret gun in that position, I shouted to the pilot, 'Dead astern,' and, after his evasive manoeuvre, I was able to fire a long burst and the Jap was too close to miss. It was not until we had landed that I realised that the enemy pilot had certainly not missed us as the rear cockpit was full of holes, with one bullet lodged in the radio instruction book beneath my feet. My hope of proving a "kill" faded when my camera-gun was found to have failed to operate!'

Also on the raid, flying with 820 Squadron, TAG, Arthur Stocker, found that,

'There were balloons which we didn't expect, plenty of flak, and Jap fighters everywhere. We dropped our bombs and turned for home, on the ground billowing smoke and flames, the raid was over in 12 minutes but it seemed to last for ever! On the way to the rendezvous, an Avenger alongside us went down in flames, it must have been the one from 857 shot down by a Tojo fighter with PO(A) D.H. Duncan as the TAG.'

At 0830, the strike force began the return trip to the fleet, arriving there, with no further enemy intervention. One Avenger, from 820, failed to return although radio messages had been picked up from it after the raid. The TAG of the crew was Leading Airman C.L. Harris, who had been "a great mate" of Arthur Stocker. A Hellcat, of the escort, also failed to return although the pilot survived but was later captured. The Avenger of 857's CO sustained damage when hit by flak and had difficulty getting back but managed to make a deck landing of sorts. His TAG, Bill Pirie, recalls,

'A hole in the starboard wing was almost big enough to put your head through and was within an inch of the main wing support. It was thought that we had been hit by a 40mm shell which, fortunately for us, had failed to explode.'

The Ramrods, consisting of 24 Corsairs, had little opposition from enemy fighters and were able to operate at will, strafing any targets on the airstrips including parked aircraft, hangars, control towers, trucks, and buildings. However, the cost was heavy, with five Corsairs being lost, mainly due to anti-aircraft fire. It appeared that they had been deployed too late to prevent most enemy fighters taking off to await the incoming strike force. The Mana strike on the airfield had been successful in wrecking the runway, but one Avenger had to turn back before the attack. With all aircraft recovered, Force 63 withdrew to the south-west.

Apart from radar contact with a small group of enemy aircraft in the afternoon, the fleet remained undetected and during the two days, 26 and 27, joined Force 69 for re-fuelling. The operation proved slow and troublesome but of greater significance than the delay was the level of remaining fuel stocks, which were sufficient for only one more strike on the refineries. The fleet turned back towards Sumatra for Operation MERIDIAN 2, for which the strike force was reduced in order to reinforce the air patrols over the fleet by 12 fighters. The full force, of 124 aircraft, comprised 48 Avengers escorted by 50 fighters, 24 fighters for Ramrod sweeps over the two major airfields, and two Fireflies for armed reconnaissance of Mana airfield. As the attack was to be on the second refinery, Soengei Gerong, the Avengers, after bombing, would make a wide sweep to starboard to form up at the previous rendezvous. The object of this change of plan was to avoid the AA batteries based at Palembang to the north although the route was longer than that used on the first raid. The problem of the balloons was also discussed by the strike leaders.

As the fleet approached the flying off position on January 29, the weather was, once again, bad with low cloud, strong winds and rainstorms making it necessary to postpone take-off until 0640. The poor visibility made forming up both difficult and time-consuming and it was almost an hour later before the strike force set out. One Avenger ditched soon after take-off while three others and four Corsairs had to return before reaching the target. After crossing the coast, the Strike Leader climbed to 13,000 feet to clear the Barisan range and started the long haul across the jungle-clad slopes of the Sumatran plain. The unwelcome news of enemy fighters reached the Avengers while still 50 miles from the target but the Top Cover fighters drove the enemy off, destroying a Tojo in the process. Reaching the refineries, where the balloons were still aloft, the Avengers deployed for their attacks and it was then that the Japanese fighters struck. In particular, they concentrated their attacks on 849, the lead squadron of No. 1 Wing, but the Avengers struggled on, dived through the flak barrages and balloons, and dropped their four 500 1b. bombs on their specific targets. No. 2 Wing suffered severe loss when the CO of 854 Squadron and his wingman, attacking under the balloons, both hit cables and crashed with the loss of all crew members including the TAGs, CPO(A) H.G.C. Stollery and Leading Airman A. Barber. Once again, as individual Avengers made their way to the rendezvous they were prey for the waiting Tojos and Oscars. Despite the efforts of the Firefly escort, which destroyed three enemy fighters for the loss of one of their own, two Avengers of 849 Squadron were shot down, the TAGs being PO(A) W.J.S. McRae and PO(A) I. Barker. But it was not all one way, two Avengers proving more than a match for the attacking Tojos when their pilots, using the Avenger's front guns, shot their adversaries down. After forming up, the strike force set out for the return flight at 0900, crossing the coast an hour later, without any further opposition from the enemy. Although most of the returning aircraft landed on safely, the stricken Avenger squadrons were hard pressed to reach the fleet and stragglers continued to arrive long after the rest had landed. Six Avengers were forced to ditch but, fortunately, the crews were sighted by units of the fleet and rescued. The Corsairs on the Ramrod sweeps failed, yet again, to catch the enemy fighters on the ground and there were few targets for them to strafe; one pilot had to bale out during the return trip but was not picked up.

Roy Gibbs, a TAG on 820 Squadron, referring to his log book entries for the raid, recalls his great dismay, on arriving over the target, to see those horrendous balloons still flying. He also remembers, sitting in the turret, bewildered by the large number of fighters hurtling around the Avenger formations making the instant identification of friend or foe almost impossible.

During the morning, there had been several attempts by the enemy to locate the fleet, all being repulsed by the CAP aircraft, and it seemed quite probable that they would eventually succeed. Just before midday, seven Sally bombers were detected at a range of 25 miles and were intercepted by patrolling Corsairs and Seafires but not before they had reached the vicinity of the fleet. The Sallys, approaching at low level, were initially thought to be carrying torpedoes but it soon became apparent that they were suicide bombers intent on attacking the carriers. By this time, the guns of the whole fleet were in action and, in the space of a few minutes, the enemy bombers had been cleared from the skies by the combined efforts of the fighters and the ships' AA fire. One unfortunate result of the latter was a number of killed and wounded on *Illustrious* caused by friendly fire from a destroyer. In the afternoon, Admiral Vian signalled the completion of Operation MERIDIAN and the fleet, after re-fuelling on the next day, steamed to the south for Australia.

Despite the fact that a third strike on the refineries had not been feasible, the raids had been a great success. Up to that time, it was understood that the Sumatran refineries, including those in the north which had been attacked earlier, provided three-quarters of the aviation fuel and tank petrol requirements of the Japanese; supplies being delivered direct to the combat areas. The cessation of these supplies, even for a few months, had a serious effect upon the enemy's ability to wage war, and output, even by the end of May, was only half the previous volume and remained so for the rest of the war. In addition to the bomb damage, the Japanese had lost 68 aircraft, either on the ground or in the air, with 7 probables, a considerable proportion of their air-fleet stationed in the area. However, the cost of these achievements had been heavy, with 16 aircraft lost in combat, 11 in ditching and 14 in deck crashes, a total of 41, involving the loss of 30 members of aircrew. The worst hit of the squadrons was 849 which lost 10 aircraft and had damage to all their participating aircrafts. These two raids proved to be the biggest undertaken by the FAA during the whole war.

For the TAGs, their experiences, during the two attacks, had given them confidence in the Avenger; its ability to withstand damage and still fly, its reputation for safe ditching, and the effectiveness of its guns as a deterrent to enemy fighters were characteristics which they could appreciate, with the prospect of the coming months of battle in the Pacific.

PALEMBANG
THE TRAGIC AFTERMATH

The great success of the Palembang raids was itself an ominous portent of the fate of any naval aircrew falling into the clutches of the Japanese. An attack by US Superfortresses, in August 1944, had prompted them to increase the defences around the refineries and it was plainly evident that the oil supplies were considered of vital importance for the prosecution of the war in the Pacific region. The immediate effect of the cutting of those supplies, to a third of normal production, must have caused a great loss of face for those Japanese officers responsible for the defence of the refineries and so the search for the culprits would have been motivated by hatred for those responsible. A measure of the frantic attempts of the Japanese to justify the apparent success of their defence of the refineries was the claims, put out by them, of the aircraft shot down, 206 plus 33 probables; in fact, more than the total complement, of 238, carried. Of the 30 aircrew missing, a proportion either baled out or made a successful forced landing and so, had a slim chance of escaping. However, although arrangements were made for contacting a submarine or a Walrus, amphibious aircraft, the possibility of escape was remote. It appears that nine aircrew, including two Avenger crews, were eventually captured and, after questioning, sent to Singapore for interrogation by the Kempei Tei, secret police, at Outram Road prison. What actually happened to them there, it has never been possible to discover but that they were brutally executed is certain, possibly by beheading on the beach at North Changi, their bodies being disposed of at sea. The date of their deaths has been put as 31st July, 1945, but it has been suggested that it may have been later, after the 15th August. On the relief of Singapore, in September, during investigations into war crimes, three Japanese officers were arrested in connection with the deaths and admitted their guilt. However, before they could be officially charged with the crime, all three committed suicide. The killing of prisoners to cover up their ill-treatment might well have been a policy by the Japanese when their surrender was imminent.

* * * *

As mentioned earlier, I had heard that my previous pilot and observer, Lt. (A) K.M. Burrenston RNVR and S/Lt (A) W.E. Lintern RNVR, had been posted missing and the appearance of their names on the FAA memorial confirmed their deaths. However, I was unaware of the manner in which they had died and it was not until 1969 that I learned the truth. I was reading John Winton's book *The Forgotten Fleet* when, on page 93, the names Burrenston and Lintern caught my eye; the discovery of their fate was, if anything, a greater shock than on the occasion of the first news, which, being wartime, made their loss regrettable but acceptable. The barbarous brutality of their actual deaths was something else and still leaves me with a lingering sense of sorrow and outrage.

Burrenston, Lintern and I had flown as a crew over 250 times and, strange to recall, I cannot bring to mind any occasions of unpleasantness, argument or disagreement, which can often arise at times of stress, and wartime flying could be demanding. Burrenston was a very competent pilot and I always had the utmost faith in his flying capabilities. He was a quiet man with a friendly nature and he encouraged me to persevere with my ambition to train as a pilot. It was probably this aspect of common interest which made for a closer relationship than that with my observer. Despite sharing the rear cabin with the observer in the early days, I found Lintern a polite but reserved person somewhat uncommunicative outside of the needs of the job. In fact, when flying there was little conversation exchanged among the crew, apart from that apposite to the particular flight, in contrast to that so often portrayed on films of RAF aircrew, who seem to spend a large part of the time with banal exchanges over the Intercom. Perhaps, we were the odd ones out? When the observer started flying in the centre cabin, he was as remote, in a way, as the pilot and rarely came back into the rear cabin, so personal contacts were fewer.

When the transfer of three crews to 849 took place in October, 1944, I assumed, at the time, that it was the result of instructions from the central drafting authority, but I was wrong. Reading the book *Avenger from the Sky* by Donald Judd, published in 1985, I discovered that the transfer was initiated by Judd himself who was the Senior Pilot on 845 at the time. It appears that he met the CO of 849 Squadron, who had been a member of his pilot's course, and was offered the chance of joining 849 as Senior Pilot which he accepted. As 849 wanted other experienced Avenger crews, Judd proposed to Burrenston and Halliday that they go with him and they agreed so arrangements were made with the FAO, East Indies, to that effect. In the event, although the observers accompanied their pilots, the TAGs did not, three less experienced TAGs being drafted but not as members of those three crews.

In 1990, the long-overdue recognition of the sacrifices made by the nine Palembang aircrew was finally put in hand. It started with an appeal to the TAG Association by the widow of Jim McRae, one of the two TAGs killed; she was asking for assistance in her attempt to have a memorial erected, at Changi, to the memory of the nine. The Association acted immediately by establishing a Changi Memorial Fund which, organised by Dickie Richardson, a TAG in the Palembang raids, attracted overwhelming response. As a result, in August 1992, following a service of dedication at Changi Prison Chapel, a Memorial Plaque was presented to the Changi Prison Museum in memory of all prisoners of war who lost their lives in captivity. In addition, a memorial stone, naming the nine aircrew, was installed in the FAA Memorial Church at Yeovilton in 1993.

The Palembang operation has now taken its place as the acme of the FAA endeavours in the Far East during World War Two. Not only was it the largest individual operation by the FAA but, also, it achieved the greatest adverse effect upon the enemy. The scale of the awards made, at the time, are indicative of that fact; seven Distinguished Service Medals were gained by TAGs, quite apart from the many other awards to pilots and observers. Its recognition has also served to bring attention to the scale of the operations undertaken by the FAA in the eastern theatre which, perhaps because of its remoteness from Europe, did not command the same news coverage. But, in any event, the US operations were so extensive in the Pacific that they dominated the news from that region. Furthermore, after VE Day, war news was no longer so important as thoughts turned to postwar problems and peace. Therefore, it is opportune that 1995 should be the fiftieth anniversary of the end of the war in the Far East and that the FAA's achievements and sacrifices, including Palembang, should be remembered at that time.

MEMBERS OF PALEMBANG AIRCREW EXECUTED

Observers	Pilots	TAGs
S/Lt(A) W.E. Lintern RNVR	Lt(A) K.M. Burrenston RNVR	PO(A) W.J.S.McRae
S/Lt(A) D.V. Roebuck RNVR	S/Lt(A) J.R. Burns RNVR	PO(A) I. Barker

(Two Crews from 849 Avenger Squadron - HMS *Victorious*)

Lt(A) E.J. Baxter RNZNVR

S/Lt(A) R.J. Shaw RNVR

(Pilots from 1833 Corsair Squadron - HMS *Illustrious*)

Lt(A) J.K. Haberfield RNZNVR

(Pilot from 1839 Hellcat Squadron - HMS *Indomitable*)

1945

Working up with *Implacable*, on passage from the UK, 828 lost a number of aircraft through ditchings but without any crew fatalities. It was later found that the loss of engine power which led to some of these losses was due to the wrong type of sparking plug being fitted. Reaching Ceylon, on 9th April, 828 flew ashore to RNAS China Bay, at Trincomalee, to continue their working-up. A few days later, Gordon Passmore, one of the TAGs, had a most memorable experience reminiscent of some far-fetched film epic which experienced fliers would deride.

'One afternoon, we were performing a high-glide bombing exercise on a towed-target off the coast at Foul Point when, while pulling out on the second bombing run, the aircraft starting banking steeply to starboard for no apparent reason. Whilst I was debating whether to bale out, the pilot announced over the intercom that he was feeling very dizzy and his vision was so blurred that he could not see his instruments. He thereupon instructed us to bale out, but with the aircraft still banking at less than 2000 feet that prospect was uninviting. After a hurried conversation with the observer, he and I suggested to the pilot that it would be more prudent to try to get the aircraft on an even keel and to fly back towards the airfield before baling out. I advised the base by radio of our predicament and our proposed plan of action. The observer gave the pilot instructions to bank either port or starboard while I kept both informed of our height, reading the altimeter in the rear cabin. In this way, we pursued an erratic course back to the vicinity of the airfield, by which time the pilot was feeling more confident of controlling the aircraft with the help of our verbal instructions. We therefore decided to attempt a crash landing and advised airfield control accordingly. With the observer directing the pilot, we flew down the duty runway at 1500 feet then, reaching the end, we banked to starboard for our final approach circuit. Having lowered wheels and flaps, the pilot continued to bank gently to starboard while losing height gradually as I called out the altimeter readings. The approach turned out so well that we decided to try a landing at the first attempt, and with the aircraft low over the runway, the observer called out "cut engine." We dropped like a stone, hitting the ground with a tremendous crash, and careered along the runway, eventually running off the concrete and coming to an impromptu stop virtually undamaged - what a trip!'

As a result of this incident, Gordon's pilot was grounded while he and his observer each joined a different crew. Less than three weeks later, when the squadron had re-embarked on *Implacable* bound for Fremantle, Gordon was involved in yet another unusual incident but this time there were tragic consequences. The squadron had taken off for a glide bombing exercise, in the vicinity of the Cocos Islands, when they were surprised by a squadron of Seafires which mounted a dummy attack.

'We had climbed to around 10,000 feet, and were preparing to launch our attack, when out of the sun a formation of Seafires burst upon us. I was in the turret at the time and saw them diving to attack. One of the Seafires picked on our sub-flight, of which our aircraft was the leader, and so I swung the turret round and watched its approach through the gunsight. As I trained the turret to follow the curving trajectory of the aircraft, I sensed that it was aiming for the Avenger which was behind and below us. The image of the Seafire in my gunsight got bigger and bigger until both it and the Avenger disintegrated before my startled gaze. I was stunned initially, but then tried to see if anyone had managed to bale out. There were reports from other aircraft of an unopened parachute plummeting down to the sea, and our aircraft was detailed off to conduct a search. After a short time, we located what looked like a head bobbing up and down in the water, and decided to drop a dinghy, mine as it happened, which entailed putting it out of the cabin door. Trying to push the door open when in flight proved to be quite a strenuous exercise, but eventually I managed to drop the dinghy as we made a low pass over the unfortunate airman below. I reported the sighting over the R/T, giving an approximate position, and we stayed in the vicinity until another Avenger replaced us, leading the ASR destroyer towards the area to effect the rescue. It was some days later, when the ship reached Fremantle, that we learned that it was the pilot of the Avenger who had survived the crash and was in relatively good shape considering all things. His observer, who was killed, had been the observer in my old crew, and less than three weeks earlier he and I had shared the experience of bringing back an Avenger with a disabled pilot. The TAG who was killed, was Leading Airman Mark Allen.'

It is interesting to note that Gordon managed to make contact with the pilot in January 1991, and they were able to acquaint each other of their side of the tragic happenings on that fateful day, 46 years previously.

After reaching Fremantle, *Implacable* sailed for Sydney where the squadron flew ashore to Jervis Bay, a satellite to Nowra, one of the main FAA bases in Australia. Here, the final preparations were made before the ship sailed for Manus, in the Admiralty Islands, towards the end of May.

* * * *

After a short stay at RNAS Trincomalee, 851 rejoined *Shah* on February 8, sailing for Durban where it underwent a refit. For this period, the squadron flew ashore to the SAAF base at Stamford Hill, where the RNAS had lodger facilities, re-embarking on April 5. The *Shah* reached Trincomalee in time to join Force 63, under the command of Vice Admiral Walker, comprising the battleships *Queen Elizabeth* and *Richelieu*, escort carriers *Empress* and *Shah*, the 5th

Cruiser Squadron and five destroyers. Their task was a covering operation, code-named BISHOP, for the amphibious operation to occupy Rangoon, code-named DRACULA; the aim being to prevent enemy interference, by either sea or air. For three days, from April 30th, the ships of Force 63 bombarded targets in the Andaman and Nicobar Islands, including airfields, coastal batteries, port installations and shipping, backed up with strafing attacks by the Hellcats from *Empress*. For the next two days, air attacks, by Avengers and Hellcats, were made on shipping and airfields along the Burma coast, after which attention was switched once again to the Andamans and Nicobars, concluding with an attack by Hellcats on the airfield at Car Nicobar. During the whole operation, enemy opposition was minimal and aircraft losses were restricted to one Hellcat hit by flak at Port Blair. Force 63 returned to Trincomalee on May 9th.

The announcement of Victory in Europe on May 8th would have provided an opportunity for celebration by the fleet on its return to port but for the signal to sail on the following morning. Intelligence reports had been received indicating that Japanese surface ships would be sailing from Singapore for the relief of their garrisons in the Andamans and Nicobars. Force 61, under the command of Admiral Walker, left port on May 10th for Operation DUKEDOM, the destruction of Japanese relief forces. Force 61 was similar in composition to Force 63 with the addition of two extra carriers from the 21st ACS and the 26th Destroyer Flotilla, which was to play a leading role in the dramatic events of the next week. The carriers included *Shah* with 851 aboard but owing to a faulty catapult the squadron had to transfer to *Emperor* with some unfortunate results.

On May 10, submarine *Subtle*, on patrol in the Malacca Strait, reported a Japanese heavy cruiser and destroyer, later identified as *Haguro* and *Kamikaze*, heading north west. Force 61 hoped to intercept on the 12th but, having been sighted by a Japanese reconnaissance aircraft, altered course to the south. In the meantime, the enemy ships, warned of the presence of Force 61, turned back to Singapore only to be sighted by *Subtle* on the morning of the 12th. The submarine attacked with torpedoes but failed to make a hit and, afterwards, had to endure severe depth-charging which inflicted considerable damage but she survived. Fortunately, a second British submarine, *Statesman*, sighted *Haguro* and signalled its southward course. Hoping that the enemy might try again, Admiral Walker remained to the south and on the 13th destroyers were re-fuelled by the escort carriers. On the 14th, Force 61 sailed west to make contact with the tanker group some two hundred miles off the northern tip of Sumatra but, in the evening, an RAF Liberator reported a Japanese supply ship with escort off the Nicobars heading south. As a result, preparations for an air and sea search were put in hand and, early on the 15th, the 26th DF was detached to begin the sea search and, later, around 0730, four 851 Avengers were launched to undertake an armed reconnaissance. The Avengers were flying separate sectors and had been briefed to report any sighting then wait for all four aircraft to rendezvous before bombing the enemy ships. Three hours later, an Avenger signalled that it had sighted the enemy ships and was going to attack; in the event, the aircraft was shot down and ditched. Meantime, four more Avengers had been launched, one of which, searching for the ditched crew, sighted *Haguro* and *Kamikaze*. They had given up a second attempt to carry out their relief mission and were at the northern end of the Malacca Strait, bound for Singapore. Preparations were put in hand to launch a strike of Avengers and, at 1355, three aircraft, all that were available at short notice, were despatched. At 1530, the Avengers attacked *Haguro* with bombs, resulting in one possible hit and one near miss. The fate of *Haguro* was now left to the 26th DF which, in a brilliant night attack, finally sank the heavy cruiser in the early hours of May 16; *Kamikaze* managed to escape to fight another day. The supply ship and escort, which shot down the lone Avenger, reached Penang safely but were both sunk in the following month. It was the last major action, using gun and torpedo, by the Royal Navy in World War Two.

Force 61 was subject to sporadic attacks by enemy aircraft later that day when one of the destroyers was damaged. It had been a frustrating time for 851 Squadron, having had two opportunities to attack enemy forces but failing to inflict any serious damage in either. The transfer of the squadron to *Emperor*, owing to the unserviceability of *Shah*'s catapult, led to handling difficulties on board which hampered operations but, in any event, the sightings made by 851 aircraft were a significant factor in the destruction of *Haguro*. This is borne out by the awards made to 851 aircrews, which for TAGs included two DSMs and two MIDs.

851 spent the next six weeks ashore, the first half of the period at RNAS Katukurunda and the second half at RNAS Colombo where, at the end of June, it re-embarked on *Shah* for strikes on Burma and Sumatra. On this occasion, the squadron was joined by four Avengers, with crews, from 845. *Shah* sailed on June 27 and, together with other carriers of the 21st ACS, carried out a series of raids on shipping, airfields, and communication systems with little opposition from the enemy. Returning to Trincomalee on July 6, 851 flew ashore to the RNAS where it remained until rejoining *Shah*, in early August, for the planned strike on Penang. 845 Squadron was also aboard *Shah* and the subsequent operations of both squadrons and their disbandment, on October 7, is described elsewhere.

*　*　*　*

On December 29, 845 moved to *Begum*, a sister ship to the *Ameer*, and I recall the day well as I was put in charge of the party unloading the stores and baggage onto the lighter for ferrying it across to *Begum*; not a job which I relished! We had only gone aboard for passage to Colombo so squadron ratings had to spend their time in the hangar but, as TAGs, we used the aircrew Ready Room which, with the air-conditioning plant operating, was quite cool and enabled us to have a reasonable night's sleep, albeit in an armchair. At Colombo, the squadron disembarked to the RNAS where we occupied new Nissen huts and not the grandstand, as on our last visit in October. It did not take long for the squadron to settle in and, during January, a comprehensive flying programme was undertaken. I was now flying with the new Senior Pilot, Lt. (A) Williams and my observer was Lt. (A) W. H. Saxon. On February 1, we were told that the squadron was going to join *Empress*, another Ruler class carrier, and we hoped that, from now on, the squadron would be usefully employed on operations against the enemy. The months since leaving *Illustrious* had been wasted and, what was then, possibly, the best trained Avenger squadron had now lost many of its experienced aircrew and had its aircraft complement reduced to eight; things could only improve!

The squadron having embarked, *Empress* sailed for Trincomalee, the aircraft flying aboard the next day. During the passage, the Wildcat flight, attached to the squadron since August, left. For the next three weeks, the ship spent most days at sea, returning to Trincomalee in the evening after the flying programme had been completed. The absence of wind at sea meant that all aircraft were launched by the steam catapult. During this period, I decided to apply once again for a pilot's course and duly put in my request to the CO who, to my surprise, granted mine but dismissed those of two other TAGs. At the time, I thought of my old pilot and the support which he had given me in my endeavours and so it was particularly saddening to hear, two days later, of the losses on the Palambang raid and that my old crew were two of those reported missing. It was much later before details of the raid became known.

On February 22, Force 62, comprising carriers *Empress* and *Ameer*, cruiser *Kenya*, three destroyers and three frigates sailed on Operation STACEY with the flag of Vice Admiral Walker aboard *Empress*. The object of the operation was photographic reconnaissance of the Malayan peninsula and surrounding areas needed for the reconquest of Malaya and Singapore. As the areas were beyond the range of most photo-reconnaissance aircraft, the East Indies Fleet undertook most of the task. 845 Avengers flew anti- submarine patrols around the Fleet while the Hellcats, of 804 on *Ameer*, provided combat air patrols. My first flight was a search for the destroyer, *Vigilant*, which had returned to Trincomalee soon after sailing but was rejoining us on the 23rd. On Sunday 25, services were held on the flight deck despite the sighting of an enemy aircraft. The next day, the P.R. Hellcats of 888 Squadron, the only specialist unit of its kind in the FAA, were launched from *Empress*. All returned safely but one crashed in the sea on landing and one Avenger hit the barrier. There was briefing for possible strikes but the reconnaissance had later revealed a lack of suitable targets. The P.R. Hellcats flew off for further reconnaissance surveys on the next two days while the Avengers continued their anti-submarine patrols. But on the second day, with the Fleet east of the Nicobars and about a 100 miles off the enemy coast, a leaflet raid was made by the CO of 845; John Munro, Chief TAG, who was on the mission recalls the occasion.

'We were boosted off at 0920 and climbed to 15,000 feet which meant using oxygen for most of the trip. As we were on our own, I spent the whole trip in the turret keeping a nervous watch on the vast expanse of clear blue sky. As we were so high, with the great expanse of empty sea below, the aircraft, despite the roaring engine, seemed to be stationary as there was nothing in sight against which to show that we were moving. The thought of being intercepted by enemy fighters was ever in your mind and, without a scrap of cloud in sight, there would be nowhere to run and hide. One thing was certain, a single Avenger was no match for even one enemy fighter. It was not a subject to dwell on but, as we flew further away from the Fleet, it was difficult not to do so. The brief was to drop the 40,000 leaflets over the Kra Isthmus of Siam, from just south of the Burmese border to the Island of Terutau, just north of Malaya. The leaflets, printed in four languages, advised the population to keep away from danger by avoiding Japanese installations and also repeated Churchill's promise to restore to China all territories stolen from the Chinese. Having completed the drop, the CO put the aircraft's nose down and made the fastest speed possible, allowing for remaining fuel. The operation took less than the four hours forecast and it is possible that we had landed before the first leaflets had reached the ground. It was nice to be back with the Fleet.'

The *Empress* went to action stations at 0230 while passing through the Nicobar Islands but it was not until 0900 that the approach of enemy aircraft was detected. The Hellcats of 804 shot down two Oscar fighters and a reconnaissance Dinah, the first Japanese aircraft to be destroyed in combat by fighters from British escort carriers. After making a partial withdrawal, the Fleet met with Force 61 and refuelling took place before turning again towards the Sumatran coast. On March 4, The P.R. Hellcats were flown off again and having returned safely, the Fleet turned for Trincomalee, arriving there three days later. Japanese radio reports of the raids claimed to have shot down a large number of our aircraft.

After a day at Trincomalee, *Empress* sailed for Colombo, where 845 went ashore to the RNAS at which messing conditions had greatly improved as a result of much new building. Leave was granted to aircrew and so John Munro, Fred Townsend and I arranged to stay at the Uva Goose club again. On this occasion, we travelled by train; arrangements with the sleeping-car attendant ensuring that we enjoyed the benefit of first-class sleeping berths. On our return, it was back to the usual flying programme of A/S bombing with, now and then, glide bombing from around 5000 feet. The POs' Board was held on March 28, from 0900 to 1500, and I passed my confirmation examination which would enable me to apply to be confirmed in the rank of PO, which had the advantage of a change of uniform from 'square rig' to 'fore and aft', thereby getting rid of the bell-bottoms and round hat. When I took to wearing the peaked cap, I recall flinging my round hat into the sea, from the flight deck of the *Empress*, to the cheers of the assembled TAGs! On March 29, the squadron embarked on *Empress* for passage to Trincomalee where, the next day, we went ashore to the RNAS. Here, the flying programme included air-firing and, on one trip, I encountered, for the first time, the "cook-off". This was the term used to describe the spontaneous discharge of a cartridge, caused by the gun overheating after firing. The gun in the turret was air-cooled but, in the tropics, this sometimes proved insufficient. In my case, the "cook-off" occurred after I had fired about a 100 rounds and was waiting for the aircraft to turn before re-commencing firing at the drogue. Normally, at this point, the turret would be returned to its normal position with the gun pointing at the aircraft's tail, in which case the discharge would put a bullet through the tail-fin and, possibly, anything else which happened to be in the firing line. In theory, the gun was incapable of being fired in such a position but that assumed that it would be fired by means of the firing-pin which, with the "cook-off", it was not. The first instance on the squadron occurred in 1944 and resulted in damage to the tail-fin but, since then, TAGs had been instructed, in such circumstances, not to return the gun to its normal position but to point it skyward while waiting for the aircraft to turn, which I had done, thus avoiding any damage. Of course, after firing was completed, even if some cartridges remained, you would pull the bolt back and withdraw the cartridge belt thus rendering the gun safe.

On April 7, the squadron was on the move again, first to *Empress* then transferring to *Emperor*, another Ruler class carrier, on the same day. The next day, *Emperor*, with the flag of Rear Admiral Patterson, sailed as part of Force 63 commanded by Vice Admiral Walker in the battleship *Queen Elizabeth*. The Force also included escort carrier *Khedive*, the French battleship *Richelieu*, cruisers *London* and *Cumberland* and five destroyers. Operation SUNFISH was intended to continue the photographic reconnaissance of Malaya and to carry out air strikes, bombardments and anti-shipping sweeps. Things did not start well when the aircraft flew aboard; I was with other TAGs watching the Hellcats of 808 land on *Khedive*, which was on our starboard beam, when one hit the rear of the flight deck, burst into flames and fell back into the sea. On *Emperor*, the Avengers landed safely but one P.R. Hellcat hit the barrier; these two incidents were but a foretaste of worse things to come. For the next two days, the Fleet sailed eastwards, with the usual patrols being flown, when, once again, we were to witness flying accidents on *Khedive*. Landings were in progress, with several Hellcats parked forward of the flight deck barrier, when the next one came in to land. The aircraft hit the deck heavily just short of the barrier and, its hook having failed to engage any of the arrester wires, the forward impetus carried it over the barrier to crash into two of the parked aircraft. A pilot and four others being killed. A most tragic event for the Hellcat squadron.

On April 11, at 0750, operations commenced with the battleships bombarding Sabang Island, off Northern Sumatra; their targets were the naval workshops, coaling sheds and commercial wharves of the port. At the same time, three destroyers attacked a port on the mainland while Hellcats strafed nearby airfields. The Japanese reacted with a number of air raids but these were broken up by the Hellcats providing the combat air patrol. Two enemy aircraft, by use of cloud cover, managed to get through and drop their bombs but these fell harmlessly in the sea. There was a tendency for the enemy aircraft to avoid combat by dodging into the clouds but one Oscar was shot down. Later, in the afternoon, a Dinah was also destroyed but in these actions, three Hellcats were damaged. The next day was given over to refuelling from Force 63 tanker and then the Fleet closed the west coast of Sumatra from which position, west of Padang, the photographic reconnaissances were to be made on the 14th and 15th. The weather over Malaya on the 14th was poor but the P.R. Hellcats took off from *Emperor* at 0730 as planned. One aircraft failed to return, due to engine failure, and its loss was made more poignant by the reports of the pilot's last radio message as he was starting to ditch. S/Lt (A) J.W. Tomlinson, an American, was rescued by a fishing boat but was later captured by the Japanese and killed. On *Emperor*, a Hellcat broke its arrester hook when landing, hit the barrier and somersaulted onto its back. Fortunately, the pilot was uninjured and the aircraft, after removal of anything of value, was pushed over the side. On *Khedive*, a Hellcat had a similar crash but damaged two others in the process; aircraft were getting scarce! In his evening address to the ship's company, the Captain mentioned that we had "crossed the line" during the day on five separate occasions.

The next day, P.R. Hellcats flew off to continue their reconnaissance of the Port Swettenham and Port Dickson areas, returning safely at 1030. There were numerous enemy alarms during the day and one Oscar was shot down and a Peggy damaged by our fighters. However, one enemy aircraft succeeded in penetrating the entire defences of the Fleet, dropping two bombs some distance from the carriers and escaping without a shot being fired - a cautionary warning of over-confidence.

The next day, action stations on *Emperor* were at 0600 in preparation for the launch of four P.R. Hellcats and the eight Avengers of 845. The latter, escorted by Hellcats from 808, flew the 80 miles to the west coast of Sumatra to bomb the port of Emmahaven. In the attack, harbour installations were damaged and a 4000 ton freighter set on fire while the Hellcats strafed the nearby airfield damaging three Dinahs on the ground and shooting down one Oscar. Two destroyers also joined in, with sweeps of the neighbouring shipping channels, looking for any targets which could be useful to the enemy. No losses were suffered and all aircraft landed safely on return. With the operation completed, the Fleet withdrew and proceeded to Ceylon. During passage, the Hellcat ground crews on *Emperor* were transferred to *Khedive* by means of the Avengers of 845. On April 18, *Emperor* left the Fleet to proceed to Colombo, arriving there two days later; the Avengers of 845 flying ashore earlier. Squadron personnel disembarked in the morning of the 21st and, having unloaded stores and baggage, went by lorry to the RNAS where, a short time after our arrival, two Hellcats crashed on take-off but, by now, such events were commonplace to us. The squadron settled down to fly a programme of miscellaneous exercises, including bombing, air-firing, beacon, navex, BALBO, but with no apparent aim in view. By this time, new crews were joining the squadron to replace ones which had been drafted and I was now flying with a number of different crews. My observer, Lt.(A) W.H. Saxon, had returned to the UK to join 736 Squadron for a TBR Air Strike Instructor's Course, during which he was killed when his Avenger's wing buckled in a steep dive. He had been most friendly and helpful to me for the few months which we had flown together and was well liked on the squadron. On May 13, our aircraft flew aboard *Empress* while the rest of the squadron joined the ship when it entered dry-dock on the following day. On that day, I took a City & Guilds examination in radio communication for which I had been studying for some months, aided by helpful squadron radio mechanics. The project had filled many hours of otherwise boring idleness even though the examination success in itself proved of no value to me. During this time, John Munro, Chief TAG, was drafted to the ship's Communication Division, pending his draft to the UK for a TAG 2 course, and I was appointed in his place. However, as it was then known that I was likely to receive a UK draft soon, the appointment was pointless. On May 21, the ship, having been fitted with a new screw, left dry-dock and put to sea bound for Trincomalee, reaching there on the next day. On May 23, both the CO, Lt/Cdr (A) J.F. Arnold, RN and Senior Observer, Lt.(A) G.M. Moffett, RNVR left the squadron; the new CO was Lt/Cdr (A) D.S. Watts, RNVR. I was now the only member of the original aircrew remaining on the squadron but only for three days, as I also received a draft chit and left on May 26.

For me, the move was something of an anti-climax as it was already apparent that the war was reaching its end and that it would be most unlikely that I should complete a pilot's training before that time. So, I felt that it might have been better to stay with the squadron for the remaining months but, on the other hand, all my contemporaries had gone and things had changed. Furthermore, I was getting a little run-down, as my recent medical had revealed, and the recurrent bouts of prickly heat, brought on by the hot humid climate, and an outbreak of boils had not improved my temper. On balance, it was probably best that I was leaving. One regret I had was that I never realised on my final trip that it would, in fact, be my last and I should have liked to have savoured the experience of what had been my 333rd flight in an Avenger. One thing which I did not appreciate, during my last 14 months on 845, was the continuous movement, from one base to another, to which the squadron was subjected. In all, we moved 18 times excluding the three visits to the Diyatalawa Rest Camp, surely some kind of record! Two days after leaving *Empress*, I went aboard the TSS *Moreton Bay* for passage to the UK, only to find that my CO and SO were also on board. I found the company of the latter, Lt. Moffett, most welcome during the dreary monotony of the three weeks' voyage home.

After I had left, the squadron continued the frenetic pattern of moves from one place to another; in early June, moving from *Empress* to RNAS Trincomalee then back to RNAS Colombo where personnel were sent on leave to Diyatalawa Rest Camp. A couple of days later, orders were received to return to Colombo, where four aircraft with crews and ground staff joined *Shah*; the rest of the squadron remaining at RNAS Colombo. The *Shah*, with 851, as the resident Avenger squadron, and the four Avengers of 845 sailed for the coast of Burma at the end of June. With other escort carriers, *Shah* carried out strikes on targets in Burma and Sumatra including shipping, airfields, and communication systems. *Shah* returned to Trincomalee where, in the middle of July, the rest of 845 went aboard, so reuniting the squadron.

One of the new TAGs joining the squadron during this time was Jim Hind, and the extraordinary manner in which he came to 845 is worthy of mention. Many strange things happened during the war, some of which, although of no great moment in themselves, remain unexplained to those involved and leave them wondering still, after 50 years, why it happened. Jim Hind finished his TAG training in Canada and crewed up at the USNAS in Maine where they completed a course on torpedo dropping. Returning to the UK, his crew joined 763, an Operational Training Squadron, at RNAS Inskip towards the end of 1944. After a few weeks there, Jim was given weekend leave and returned to his home at Arbroath where he received a telegram stating that he was required to report to 100 Buckingham Palace Road, London, on the next day, for service abroad. As there was no identifying authority on the telegram apart from "Your obedient servant", he was most suspicious, thinking that perhaps it was a hoax. Consequently, he reported to RNAS Arbroath for advice, asking the Officer of the Day there to confirm the authenticity of the telegram, but he refused and so Jim asked to speak to the Camp Commander. This request brought rapid action and, within the hour, he was kitted out and provided with travel warrants for his journey. Reporting to London, he was then sent on to Poole Harbour where he boarded a Sunderland Flying Boat bound for the Far East. Developing engine problems, the Sunderland landed on the Nile near Cairo where the passengers were billeted at Shepheard Hotel for repairs to be carried out. While there, it emerged that the flight was rated as top priority and this disclosure left Jim wondering exactly why his presence was so urgently required, what possible mission was he about to be involved in? This was the stuff which dreams are made of and his mind was constantly puzzling over the meaning of it all, conjuring up numerous scenarios and then dismissing them as impossible. After a week of luxury living, the journey was continued, first to Basra, then Karachi, and finally Colombo where he was once again billeted in a smart hotel. The next morning, he departed for RNAS Colombo, which was on the site of the old racecourse, still wondering what his destiny would be. When he reported to the RPO, his dreams dissolved as reality returned when he was told that no-one knew of his coming, where he was to go, or for what purpose! He was advised that, after completing his drafting routine, he should collect a bed from stores as he would be sleeping on the terraces of the grandstand. The last word of advice offered was, "Mind the wild dogs that roam around there." It was some months before Jim Hind joined 845 Squadron on *Shah* and he never did discover the reason for his VIP treatment on that top priority journey to nowhere!

On *Shah*, preparations began for the planned strike on Penang together with the other CVEs of the 21st Aircraft Carrier Squadron. Early in August, the Fleet sailed for Penang but, on August 6, the first news of the dropping of the atomic bomb on Hiroshima reached them. On *Shah*, Paul Tipney, who had recently joined 845 Squadron as a TAG, was looking forward to his first flight from a carrier but, when it came on August 8, the experience was not quite what he had expected it to be. He was in the turret, as the Avenger roared down the deck for take-off, and quickly became aware that the aircraft seemed to be veering to port. His assumption was proved correct when it ran off the deck, hitting the Oerlikon gun on the port sponson with its wheels, before crashing into the sea. As the port wing hit the water first, escape from the turret, with the quick-release panel on that side, was made easier. The robust construction of the Avenger prevented its breaking-up and it remained afloat long enough for the three crew members to get out, release the dinghy, and climb aboard. There was a moment of panic when the aircraft started to sink and they realised that the dinghy was still attached, but quick work by the observer, in cutting the retaining rope, saved the day. They were picked up by the cruiser *Royalist* and, after a tot in the Wardroom, returned aboard *Shah*. On Paul's next flight, which was a beacon exercise, the aircraft was boosted off and, after an uneventful trip, he recorded his first, and only, deck landing.

On August 9, the dropping of the second atomic bomb, on Nagasaki, was announced and although, in many minds, this presaged the early surrender of the enemy, preparations for the strike went on. On the 11th, with the Fleet deployed for the attack, orders were received that the attack was cancelled. Jim Hind, TAG on 845, was actually on the catapult, with his Avenger bombed up and ready to go, when the negative flag was raised and take-off delayed. After an hour's wait, the cancellation order came through and the Fleet turned back to Trincomalee. On arrival in port, the announcement of the Japanese surrender was received and, as Jim Mackenzie, Senior Radio Mechanic, recalls, 'A wild night ensued with all available pyrotechnics being shot off.'Next day, contrary to expectations, the Fleet sailed again to undertake Operation ZIPPER, the support of landings at Port Dickson and Port Swettenham in Malaya, however, the covering air and sea bombardment had been cancelled. Prior to this, two other smaller Operations, TIDERACE and JURIST, the occupation of Singapore and Penang, were to be carried out. Unfortunately, on August 19, serious delays were occasioned when General MacArthur ordered that no surrenders or landings were to be effected until he had signed the main surrender in Tokyo at the end of the month. This meant that the Fleet had to remain at sea, taking shelter from the south west monsoon, by anchoring off the Great Nicobars until orders were received to proceed. However, *Shah* and *Stalker* with some escorts returned to Trincomalee for fuel.

At Trincomalee, 845 disembarked to the RNAS and proceeded to dispose of all squadron stores and aircraft and then, with personal kit only, re-embarked for passage to the UK, on September 9. Accompanying 845 on the trip was 851 Squadron although the personnel of both were, in effect, merely passengers. The ship was carrying hundreds of returning troops and civilians who were accommodated on the hangar deck but were probably better off than being on a crowded merchant ship. The *Shah* arrived at Gourock, on the Clyde, on October 7, 1945, the official date of disbandment for both 845 and 851 Squadrons.

And I suppose bowline will be replaced by the American granny.

PACIFIC OCEAN

OPERATION ICEBERG

After fuelling, on January 30, Force 63 proceeded south to Australia, arriving Fremantle on February 4 and Sydney on the 10th. The scale of the welcome for the British Pacific Fleet was overwhelming and the people of Sydney provided unstinting hospitality both privately, in their homes, and at the British Centre, specially built for the purpose by public subscription. The squadrons had flown ashore to Nowra, an RAAF airfield loaned to the FAA as its main base for the duration, located some 70 miles south of Sydney. Roy Gibbs remembers it as,

> '...one main street and a pub. I was in the flight of 820 Squadron designated as the Torpedo Flight and we were not amused to be flying practice torpedo attacks while the rest of the lads were living it up in Sydney. But, after a week or so, we were given leave and were able to enjoy the great hospitality offered in Sydney.'

At this time, the future of the BPF was still undecided but permission was granted for the Fleet to sail to Manus, in the Admiralty Islands. The first to go was the Fleet Train, a motley collection of ships of every type and nationality, which had been assembled in great haste to be ready for when the BPF sailed to join the US Fleet. Its purpose was to provide all the supplies and service requirements of the main fleet to enable it to remain at sea for weeks at a time. Since the advent of steam, the Royal Navy had relied on a series of bases throughout the world where ships could put in for fuel and supplies thus reducing the time at sea to days rather than weeks. In the vast expanses of the Pacific ocean, this mode of operation had to change and the Fleet Train was the only viable solution in the short term. On February 24, the initial group of ships constituting the Fleet Train sailed for Manus followed, on the 27th, by the main fleet, with Vice Admiral Rawlings in command. Here, in the vast anchorage, the BPF waited, sweltering in the hot humid climate, for its orders as to what its future role was to be. Finally, on March 15, the signal came to report to Admiral Nimitz, C-in-C Pacific, for duties in connection with Operation ICEBERG which was the invasion of Okinawa, planned for April 1.

The role of BPF was not directly concerned with the invasion itself but was the subsidiary one of stopping the Japanese using the Sakishima Gunto islands, situated between Okinawa and Formosa, for sending aircraft reinforcements to the former; the main targets were to be the airfields on the main islands of Ishigaki Shima and Miyako Shima. The BPF sailed for Ulithi, in the Carolines, where it became Task Force 57 under the operational control of Admiral Spruance's US Fifth Fleet.

Task Force 57 sailed on March 18, reaching Ulithi, an atoll in the Carolines with a huge natural harbour, two days later. Here, part of the expeditionary force for the assault on Okinawa was assembled; an awe-inspiring sight for members of the BPF and indicative of the scale of the forthcoming battle of which they were to be a part. Admiral Rawlings and his staff conferred with Admiral Nimitz's Chief of Staff regarding the BPF's role in the coming conflict and received final operational orders. On the 23rd, Task Force 57 sailed for the Sakishima Gunto, refuelling on the 25th before reaching the flying-off point for the first mission early the next day.

The fleet was 100 miles south of the island of Miyako when, at sunrise, the first Ramrod of Corsairs and Hellcats was launched for a sweep of the two main islands of Ishigaki and Miyako. This was followed by two Avenger attacks when all airfields were bombed and strafed. One Avenger from 854 was shot down by AA fire over Ishigaki, the TAG was PO(A) J. Brown. The following day, having returned to the same flying-off position, a fighter Ramrod was flown off to strafe Ishigaki, followed once again by two bombing and rocket attacks, by Avengers and Fireflies. On this occasion, it was the airfields on Miyako which were attacked and, for a second time, an Avenger of 854 was hit by flak, setting a wing on fire. The pilot, CO of the squadron, attempted to extinguish the flames but the wing later collapsed and he was forced to bale out over the sea. He was picked up by a US submarine some hours later but the other crew members did not survive; the TAG was PO(A) P.H. Firth. The Strike Leader on the morning raid, CO of 857, was forced to ditch on the way back but he and his crew were picked up by the destroyer *Undine* and returned to the *Indomitable* by breeches-buoy. At the end of the day, the fleet withdrew some 200 miles to meet the Fleet Train for replenishment of stores and fuel. The actions over the two days had resulted in the loss of 17 aircraft and 9 aircrew, including 4 Avengers and 5 of their crew members. For 854 Squadron, in particular, it had been a grim beginning.

The loss of one of the Avengers on the 26th occurred when making its landing approach after returning from a raid. Aircraft crashes are, by their very nature, unique even though they may follow a similar pattern but, on this occasion, there was a truly unique element in the crash. The aircraft hit the round-down heavily, bounced, missing all the arrester wires, and shot over the port side by the 4.5 gun sponson. The TAG was Bill Jones serving with 820 Squadron on the *Indefatigable*.

'It was an easy matter to push out the escape panel of the turret, climb out onto the port wing, inflate my Mae West, and slip into the water. My pilot and observer had got out on the starboard wing and, with the aircraft sinking rapidly, had joined me in the sea as the carrier steamed away. Hearing a cry to my left, I looked round and saw a fourth person in the water and shouted to ask if he was OK. He shouted back, "I can't swim," and so I swam over to support him. By now the aircraft had disappeared and the other two crew were swimming towards us. My observer blurted out, almost accusingly, "Where the hell did he come from?" He told us that he was a member of the gun crew who, seeing our Avenger's propeller bearing down on him, had chosen the Pacific Ocean despite his inability to swim. We were soon picked up by the attendant destroyer, *Quiberon* (RAN), where the gunner and I spent the intervening days, until the next oiling, on a very crowded messdeck where we were treated with great kindness by the Aussie sailors.'

Closely following this crash, Bill survived two others, one when his aircraft hit the island and the other when it crashed into the second barrier and burst into flames. It is interesting to note that Bill was in touch with an ex-member of the *Quiberon* in 1993 and the exchange of letters between them showed the depth of the camaraderie which still exists after 50 years.

Serving with Bill Jones on 820 Squadron was a great friend of his, TAG, Chuck Sage, who was a talented cartoonist spending many hours of his free time aboard ship on his drawings. Although presented in a humorous manner, the drawings, with their trenchant comments, provided acute observations on life with the BPF. A selection of his cartoons are illustrated elsewhere in the book.

With the invasion of Okinawa due to commence on April 1, L-Day, it was. essential that raids should be mounted on the Japanese airfields over that period so, at dawn on March 31, TF 57 was on station for another strike day. it started with fighter Ramrods and CAPs over both main islands followed, during the day, by two escorted Avenger bombing raids on the airfields and barracks of Ishigaki. One Avenger of 849 Squadron was hit by flak and crashed on the airfield killing the crew; the TAG was Leading Airman N. Hewkin. So ended the third strike day but new dangers were awaiting the whole fleet on the morrow.

On one of the Avenger strikes that day, the CO of 857 was forced to ditch for the second time in two raids. He had made a good bombing run through heavy ground fire but, on the return trip, it soon became apparent that there was an oil leak and ditching was inevitable. TAG, Bill Pirie, remembers the occasion very well,

'The ditching was perfect and we were soon in the dinghy, almost without getting our feet wet. As we were near to land, there were no rescue destroyers at hand to pick us up and the outlook was far from pleasant. Sitting there, pondering our fate, we suddenly became aware of a vessel in the distance flying a flag which looked horribly like "the rising sun". For the next few minutes, as the vessel approached, the strain became unbearable but then, straining our eyes, we made out the outline of "the stars and stripes" and our relief was unbounded; it was a submarine, the USS *Kingfish*.

'Despite the lack of accommodation for passengers, we were made very welcome and the food, compared with that on the *Indomitable*, was superb. Sleeping arrangements were on the basis of one hundred percent occupation, that is, as one person got out of a bunk another got in. It so happened that one member of the crew was ill and so I volunteered to carry out his duties. I did surface lookout duties, operated the paravanes, and sat in with the telegraphists; watches were four hours on and four off. After 15 days aboard, we were put ashore at Saipan, in the Marianas, when I was presented with the submarine Dolphin Badge and a signed photograph of the crew, souvenirs which I still treasure. Our next move was a flight to Guam where, having been fitted out with US marine uniforms, we were presented to Admiral Nimitz as the first RN personnel to be rescued by a US submarine. Then, after all the excitement of the past few weeks, we were flown to Leyte to rejoin the *Indomitable* on April 17. There, I found that, on the assumption of my not returning to the ship, my kit had been packed and my two bottles of pusser's rum, which I had been saving up, had been enjoyed by the other TAGs!'

At dawn on April 1, with the first Ramrods despatched to Ishigaki, enemy aircraft were detected approaching the fleet. The Ramrods were recalled and they, together with the fleet CAP, engaged the intruders, of which two were shot down. However, some enemy aircraft eluded the covering fighters and one Oscar strafed the deck of the *Indomitable*, killing one man and injuring six others. Then, it was the *Indefatigable*'s fate to be the first target in the BPF for a kamikaze which crashed near the ship's island, killing eight men and injuring twenty-two others, six of whom later died. The damage caused was light, thanks to the armoured deck, and within the hour aircraft were landing on - a remarkable achievement which impressed the US Liaison Officer aboard. Just after noon, 16 Avengers, with Corsair escort, were launched for an attack on the airfields on Ishigaki, followed, later in the afternoon, by Ramrods which destroyed three aircraft on the ground but lost one Corsair. Bogeys were again detected at 1730 and four kamikazes, eluding the fleet CAP, attacked the fleet which sustained no damage although *Victorious* only avoided being hit by skilful evasive action on the part of Captain Denny. It had been quite an eventful day for TF 57 and, also, for the Americans who had established a firm bridgehead on Okinawa by nightfall on L-Day.

The dawn Ramrod, on the next day, discovered little evidence of enemy presence and so it was decided to withdraw the TF for refuelling, but bad weather, on the 3rd, delayed the start until the following day. Although the operation was still incomplete by the evening, the TF had to leave in order to be on station for dawn operations on the 6th. Early surveillance of the main islands revealed that the airfield runways had been repaired during the nights when the enemy could work uninterrupted. The lack of night operating aircraft meant that the task of cratering the runways had to be repeated over and over. It is hard to understand the reason for this shortcoming in night flying capacity when it is recalled that 853 Squadron was night flying from escort carriers in the autumn of 1944. Early in the afternoon, Avengers were launched to bomb Miyako airfields while the accompanying fighters strafed communication centres; there were no losses from enemy action but one Avenger ditched after take-off. In the late afternoon, some enemy aircraft were detected, intercepted and a Judy shot down but another, emerging from the clouds, dived on *Illustrious*. The ship's gunners hit the aircraft but it continued its downward plunge and only the avoiding action by *Illustrious* prevented the kamikaze from hitting its target. As it was, the explosion near the starboard side destroyed two Corsairs on deck but there were no casualties. Enemy aircraft continued to circle the fleet and three were shot down by a combination of the patrolling fighters and the destroyers' guns. The next day, Avenger strikes once again rendered the airstrips unserviceable after the previous night's repairs by the enemy. Meantime, fighters carried out their usual strafing attacks at the cost of three Corsair pilots, showing that the enemy gunners were still very effective despite the continuous bombing and strafing. TF 57 then withdrew for refuelling during the next two days.

Over the previous few days, the Americans on Okinawa had been subjected to massive air assaults, involving a total of nearly 700 aircraft, and, although they had succeeded in shooting down over half that number, had sustained heavy losses in shipping, with six sunk and over twenty damaged, including the carrier *Hancock*. In addition to the air attacks, the Japanese Navy C-in-C committed the great battleship *Yamato*, escorted by a cruiser and eight destroyers, to a "death or glory" attack in support of the besieged Okinawa. The US TF 58 disposed of this threat by sending almost 400 aircraft to bomb and torpedo the Special Attack Force which, without air cover, was completely overwhelmed; only four destroyers survived to return to Japan. The news of these great actions made the Sakishima operations by TF 57 seem very commonplace and so the receipt of orders to switch their attacks to airfields in Formosa was welcomed.

* * * *

The strikes on the Formosan airfields was code-named Operation OOLONG and on April 11, TF 57 was on station but, owing to bad weather, the operation was postponed until the next day when two Avenger strikes were launched at 0715. The first, with 820 and 857 Squadrons, bombed the airfield at Schinchiku where they were met by heavy flak but no airborne opposition. The second, with 849 and 854 Squadrons, finding Matsuyama airfield under a blanket of cloud, had to divert to the alternative target at Kiirun, where the docks and shipping were bombed. One Corsair and one Avenger from 849 failed to return from the operation; the Avenger TAG was Leading Airman G.P. Claughan. During the remainder of the day, the fleet CAPs had their most successful day to date, shooting down 14 enemy aircraft which had attempted to approach the Fleet. Before daybreak on the next day, enemy aircraft attacked the Fleet but did no damage, one being shot down by gunfire; a second attempt was intercepted and two Zekes shot down. Soon after, two Avenger strikes were launched on the same targets as the previous day but, on this occasion, both airfields, at Schinchiku and Matsuyama, were bombed; no enemy fighters put in an appearance and no aircraft were lost. With Operation OOLONG completed, TF 57 withdrew to replenish supplies and refuel.

At Okinawa, the Americans were still subject to heavy air attacks on their fleet with the consequent loss of a destroyer and damage to other ships including two battleships. So as to relieve the pressure on the US Fleet, Admiral Rawlings offered to extend the period of attacks on the Sakishima Gunto and the offer was accepted by the US Admiral Spruance. TF 57 started refuelling on the 14th and *Illustrious* left for Leyte, being replaced by *Formidable* newly arrived after her lengthy stay at Gibraltar for repairs. On board were 848 Avenger Squadron and two squadrons of Corsairs.

Illustrious, with 854 and her two Corsair squadrons aboard, left Leyte on May 4, and sailed for Sydney via Manus. TAG, Jack Gardiner, had joined 854 at Hawkinge in July, 1944, and the dawn anti-submarine patrol, on the 6th, was to be the last squadron flight for his crew, which had been flying together for two years. Therefore, it was not surprising that his was one of the Avenger crews which stayed aboard when the ship arrived at Sydney on the 14th. The remaining crews went ashore to Nowra, the RAAF base used by the FAA, where the squadron remained until October when it returned to the UK, disbanding on December 8. In the meantime, Jack Gardiner enjoyed a "holiday cruise back home" aboard *Illustrious* which eventually had its long-overdue refit. Jack has kept in touch with his crew members, Monty Montefiore and Dick Temple, ever since.

* * * *

On April 15, TF 57 returned to its old flying-off position and commenced its familiar operational pattern of strikes and CAPs. The Japanese had repaired all the runways on the six airfields so, over the next two days, seven strikes by escorted Avengers and Fireflies rendered them unserviceable yet again. This achievement was not without losses; an Avenger, from 857, was hit by flak over Hegina, the TAG being PO(A) L.A. Mellard, while a second Avenger, from 848, crashed into the sea off Hirara, the TAG was PO(A) C.W. Irvine. In addition, two fighters were shot down, one Hellcat from *Indomitable* and one Corsair from *Formidable*. In the latter case, the pilot was the CO of 1842 Squadron on his first day of operations over Sakishima. Four enemy aircraft were intercepted and destroyed by CAP fighters during the day. TF 57 then withdrew for refuelling before returning, on April 20, for the final day of ICEBERG, Phase One. Four Avenger strikes, accompanied by rocket-firing Fireflies, were launched, during which all airfields on both of the main islands were bombed and strafed, leaving them unserviceable. One 848 Avenger ditched off Ishigaki but the crew were picked up by a US air-sea rescue aircraft. With operations complete, TF 57 set course for Leyte, arriving there on the 23rd; it had been at sea for 32 consecutive days, a record for any British fleet since Nelson's day. During 12 strike days, air groups had lost 47 aircraft, 19 to flak and 28 to operational causes, with 29 aircrew killed or missing but the main aim of the Operation had been achieved - the enemy had been prevented from using their Sakishima airfields. In the course of this success, the TF had destroyed 33 enemy aircraft in the air and 12 on the ground.

The Fleet Train had now some 60 ships at Leyte and the fleet wasted no time in replenishing its vast range of necessary supplies, ranging from food to aircraft. *Indefatigable*, in particular, made good use of the services of the repair ships, which restored her to full operational capacity within the week. In the tropical heat, conditions below decks were most enervating and personnel were faced with working long hours to complete all outstanding tasks before the Fleet set sail. At dawn, on May 1, TF 57 sailed for Sakishima to take up the challenge of Operation ICEBERG yet again. On the 3rd, after final refuelling with supporting tankers, the Fleet proceeded to the flying-off position, south of Miyako, for the first of the next series of raids on the airfields. At dawn on the following day, the first CAP was dispatched and found that runways on some airfields had been made serviceable since the raids by the US TF 52 on the previous day. Two escorted Avenger strikes were launched, the first against Miyako and the second, two hours later, against Ishigaki. Heavy anti-aircraft fire was encountered and an Avenger from 857 was hit, crashing into the sea and killing the crew of which the TAG was P.O(A) L.R. Denton.

One of the crews of 820 on the first Avenger strike that morning was TAG, Roy Gibbs and his pilot and observer, Alan Ryman and Frank Burgess. As they approached the target, Roy decided to man the 0.3 Browning belly gun and fire a few bursts as they pulled out of the dive.

"I had hardly squeezed the trigger when there was a loud explosion, the plane seemed to stagger and then started to dive steeply to port with flames enveloping the starboard side. Telling myself to keep calm, I grabbed my parachute, clipped it on my harness, and pulled the ejection handle on the cabin door. Nothing happened and blind panic took over as I kicked and hammered at the door but to no avail. Suddenly, with the panic subsiding, I realised that we were flying straight and level and that the wing fire was now out; the side-slipping manoeuvres, which had so alarmed me, had been taken deliberately by the pilot to blow out the fire. There were a few small fires in the cabin which I put out and then turned my attention to the radio which had suffered from the debris blown in by the explosion. After replacing a few wires, I found, to my amazement, that the radio had started to function and so we were in contact with each other again. The pilot told me that we had been hit in the starboard petrol tank, hence the fire, and that there was a large hole in the area of the wing bolt, furthermore, the observer, being in the centre cabin and near the point of impact, had been wounded. It was not encouraging news for our trip back to the ship but fortune smiled upon us when an Avenger appeared alongside and escorted us back. As we approached the ship to land on, the pilot warned us of a rough landing to come as, with the hydraulics out, he was unable to lower the flaps or get more than the one wheel down. As regards the starboard wing he added, "It's only the heat of the fire which has welded it together." Nevertheless, he still caught the second wire and inevitably, with only the starboard wheel down, the aircraft slewed to port but otherwise it was a perfect landing. Incredibly, as we came to a stop, the cabin door, which I had been unable to jettison, fell off! After a visit to the Sick Bay, for a quick medicinal brandy, we went for the debriefing, when I suddenly remembered my gear left in the kite. I rushed on deck but was too late, it had been pushed over the side. But next day, we were flying as usual!'

The morning strike had shown that the enemy AA fire was still as lethal as ever, so the decision was taken to bombard the airfields of Miyako as conditions were favourable for that type of operation. At 1000, the bombardment force of the two capital ships, five cruisers and a destroyer flotilla steamed north, with CAP and spotting aircraft above. Two hours later, some eight miles off shore, the bombardment commenced and shortly afterwards the first signal was received telling of an attack by kamikazes on the carriers. As a result, the bombardment was curtailed and the force turned back to rejoin the carriers at maximum speed.

In the meantime, the two carriers, with their eight escorting destroyers, had been the target for several groups of suicide bombers, starting at around 1100. Although intercepted by CAP, a number of the enemy managed to break through and one, diving from the clouds, hit *Formidable* in the middle of the flight deck where aircraft had been ranged prior to flying off. These aircraft were destroyed or set ablaze, the island, bridge, and barriers damaged by the blast, while the initial impact of the bomb had penetrated the armoured deck and blown steel fragments through the hanger to the boiler-room below, severing a steam pipe and thus leading to a reduction in speed. Casualties were high, with eight killed and nearly fifty injured, some of which suffered serious burns from the raging fires on deck. A few minutes later, *Indomitable* was attacked but escaped serious damage when the aircraft, having hit the deck, plunged over the side into the sea where its bomb exploded. A little while later, yet another attempt was made on *Indomitable* but the aircraft was shot down and crashed in the sea alongside. For the next two hours, enemy aircraft continued to approach the carriers but were successfully repulsed. With the return of Admiral Rawlings and his bombardment force, TF 57 withdrew southwards to allow *Formidable* time to re-organise her flight deck which was completed by 1700 when her captain signalled that she was ready to land on aircraft; a remarkable achievement considering the damage sustained. So ended an eventful day, nine enemy aircraft had been shot down by CAP and a number by the guns of the Fleet. However, a lesson had been learnt; the carriers were very vulnerable to air attack despite the CAPs. The absence of the capital ships and cruisers had reduced the radar detection facilities and, of more importance, the AA fire-power, factors which the enemy had exploited. The armoured decks had proved their worth yet again!

At dawn on the following day, the TF was back to fly off more strikes to bomb the airfields but, on this occasion at least, the response from the enemy gun positions was extremely muted, no doubt due to the bombardment of the previous day. Apart from the shooting down of a Zeke by the dawn CAP of Corsairs, there was little enemy air activity, so the TF withdrew for refuelling and replenishment of supplies, especially replacement aircraft. On the 8th, the plans for a bombardment and bomber strikes had to be cancelled owing to bad weather conditions but the next day would find the Fleet engaged once again in a desperate battle with the kamikazes.

Despite the announcement of the end of the war in Europe, there was no time for celebration in the BPF; May 9 was just another day in the battle of attrition over the Sakishima Gunto. During the day, four bombing strikes were made, rendering all the runways unserviceable once again. In the afternoon, five enemy aircraft were detected approaching the fleet and successfully intercepted by the

Seafire CAP. Although one Zeke was shot down, the others managed to evade their pursuers and continued to close at speed. The first of the suicide aircraft dived on the *Victorious* and, despite being hit by AA fire, crashed onto the deck forward of the island, damaging the catapult, a 4.5-inch gun turret, and the lift. A second aircraft followed with an attack from the stern and, although set on fire by the barrage from *Victorious*, hit the flight deck and its blazing wreckage crashed over the side, destroying the parked Corsairs in its path. Yet a third aircraft approached the *Victorious* but was hit and crashed near *Howe*, the next in line. The fourth kamikaze attacked *Formidable* from astern and, though hit again and again, managed to dive onto the after-deck, destroying the parked Corsairs and an Avenger. The explosion caused a fire in the hangar below which, with the water used to put it out, damaged a dozen more aircraft. Despite the material damage, casualties were light, with one rating killed and several injured but, on *Victorious*, the two attacks had killed three and wounded nineteen.

Although TF 57 was still operational, *Formidable* and *Victorious* were unable to provide more than a token force of aircraft owing to the damage sustained in the suicide attacks. It was, therefore, decided to withdraw to refuel, replenish supplies, especially aircraft, and repair damage, returning for further strikes on the 12th. During this interval, at a conference of senior officers, the problem of countering the kamikaze attacks was discussed and new measures devised for increasing the fire-power brought to bear on the attackers as soon as they came within range. The recent actions had shown that the TF had insufficient fire-power to destroy the aircraft in flight.

On the 12th, the TF was stationed at its new flying-off position, a hundred miles to the south-east of Miyako Shima, ready for further offensive action against the airfields where some, at least, of the runways were again serviceable. Four strikes were made, involving nearly a hundred aircraft, bombing the runways and anything else which provided a target of use to the enemy. The CO of one of the Hellcat squadrons was shot down by ground-fire, showing that the Japanese gunners were still a serious threat despite the continual battering which they had received over the past weeks. Again, the next day, the Avengers, Fireflies, Hellcats and Corsairs were back over the islands, handing out more of the same, after which the fleet withdrew to meet up with their Support Group for replenishment. While here, Admiral Rawlings signalled Admiral Spruance regarding the future deployment of TF 57 and proposed that its operations on the Sakishima Gunto should finish on May 25; this was agreed by the USN Admiral. The news that their two month campaign would soon be over came as a great relief to all and not least to the aircrews, who were all beginning to feel the strain of the unremitting battle of attrition. There was also the need for the fleet to be made ready for a second period of operations in enemy waters.

On May 16, TF 57 was back on station and strikes were launched on the usual targets, enemy aircraft were scarce, both on the ground and in the air, but the flak was as heavy and accurate as ever. One Avenger from 820 was hit as it made a second approach to release its 1600lb bomb. The observer was badly wounded in the leg and, as the radio had been damaged, the pilot, on rejoining his squadron, had to communicate their predicament, by hand signals, to the crew of the aircraft flying alongside. Another Avenger then accompanied him back to the fleet where he was given priority to land on at once. The TAG, Ben Pearce, had in the meantime left the turret and crawled into the mid-section cockpit to attend the wounded observer who, despite Ben's efforts, succumbed to wounds later in the day. On the following day, three strikes were flown to maintain the unserviceability of the runways while, on their strafing missions, the fighters spotted and targeted a group of enemy soldiers. In the afternoon of that day, *Victorious* was forced to stop operating aircraft owing to a number of crash landings which destroyed the barriers and, in the process, damaged several aircraft. A Corsair pilot, and two members of the flight deck party were killed and several injured as a result of the crashes. On the 18th, TF 57 rejoined the Support Group for replenishment but even here, out of operational contention, misfortune was still at hand. On *Formidable*, a Corsair's guns were fired, by accident, in the hangar, causing an explosion and subsequent fire which was only extinguished by extensive spraying; the result was thirty aircraft damaged, some beyond repair.

The 20th found TF 57 back at its flying-off position for more strikes but, at dawn, just as the fleet was preparing for flying stations, it entered a belt of fog, causing the destroyer, *Quilliam*, to ram the *Indomitable*. Amazingly, the carrier was undamaged, although the destroyer suffered damage to her bows and had to be taken in tow. After a few hours, the visibility improved sufficiently for the first strike to be launched, although the cloud cover still made it difficult to reach the target but, taking advantage of a break in the clouds, the Avengers and Fireflies attacked Hirara town on Miyako. One Corsair was shot down and ditched but the pilot did not survive. The following two strikes were cancelled and the fourth had to be recalled because of the weather. On the next day, the weather gradually improved and five strikes were successfully completed, *Indefatigable* notching up a record number of sorties amounting to 94. In the afternoon, the last enemy aircraft to be shot down by the TF during Operation ICEBERG was claimed by a Hellcat. The fleet then withdrew for replenishment for the final two days of operations but *Formidable* was to retire before the end, sailing early to Sydney for extensive repairs of battle damage.

The final two days of strikes, May 24 and 25, were something of an anti-climax; seven strikes being made against the six airfields and their surrounding targets with no response from the enemy in the air and, fortunately, no losses suffered. In the evening, the TF withdrew for the last time, sailing southwards for Manus and then Sydney.

Apart from the week's break at Leyte, TF 57 had been at sea for over two months during which time, on 23 strike days, a total of nearly 5,000 sorties had been flown. Aircraft operational losses totalled around 100, involving 37 aircrew killed or missing, including 7 TAGs. However, the number of aircraft lost from all causes was over 200 out of a total complement of 218. In addition to these losses by the squadrons, there were those sustained by the five carriers from the kamikaze attacks, both as regards personnel and material damage to the ships. Compared with such losses, the achievements would appear small, 57 enemy aircraft destroyed, airfields wrecked and many subsidiary targets damaged but, of course, the primary aim of Operation ICEBERG was to prevent the enemy using the airfields for the reinforcement of their forces in Okinawa and this had been achieved. Admiral Spruance signalled his appreciation of the fine work done by the TF and reported that the BPF was ready to take its place with the Fast Carrier Task Force in future operations. For the US forces in Okinawa, their task was not over, as enemy resistance did not cease until the end of June.

In early June, the BPF arrived in Sydney, where the task of replenishing supplies and stores began at the same time as the extensive repairs of battle damage to the carriers was put in hand. However, ships' companies and squadron personnel were granted leave to enjoy the magnificent hospitality offered by the Australian people via their British Centre in Sydney. On returning from leave, some of the aircrews, who had been in the thick of the action for some months, were drafted to less demanding postings. One such person was TAG, Arthur Stocker, who had joined 820 Squadron from 852 after the *Nabob* was torpedoed in August 1944. Arthur had since been on 31 strikes against the Japanese - no mean record - and he was just one of many. The replacement crews had to be incorporated into the revised squadron organisations and this meant more training in the little time available before the BPF returned to take their place in the operations off Japan.

RAIDS ON JAPAN

Implacable had arrived at Manus in early June and was to be the flagship of Task Group 111.2, its other units comprising CVE *Ruler*, four cruisers and five destroyers; formed for the purpose of attacking Truk, the Japanese naval stronghold in the Caroline Islands. Code named Operation INMATE, its primary aim was to provide battle experience for the new units joining the BPF while, at the same time, neutralising any enemy positions which might prove a threat to Allied Forces in the area. While there, *Implacable*'s Air Staff solved the problem of the Seafire's limited range when it discovered that the fitting of a Kittyhawk drop tank, in place of the normal long-range tank used, had great advantages in the combat role. A supply of tanks was obtained via informal channels.

On June 6, prior to the commencement of INMATE, 828

Avengers, on *Implacable*, took part in a night intruder operation on Towi Island located between Manus and Truk. The plan was for two Avengers to take off every two hours throughout the night; at the target, each aircraft would make its bombing run by the light of flares dropped by the other aircraft. TAG, Gordon Passmore was in one of the Avengers that night.

'We took off just before midnight, some 50 miles from the target, and after successfully completing our final bombing run, we set course for home. Suddenly, we were subjected to a most violent buffeting and I realised from the water cascading around the fuselage that somehow we had flown into the sea. Fortunately, all three of us were well strapped-in and so escaped injury from the violence of the impact, although the pilot went down quite a distance before releasing himself from the cockpit. It transpired that after the final run, possibly due to the intensity of the flares, the pilot had lost his horizon temporarily and flown into the sea.

'Luck was with us, as sea conditions were calm and the aircraft dinghy popped out of its storage and inflated automatically, so we were soon aboard. We had also retrieved the emergency supplies, and so sent up our first distress rocket, and thereafter one every hour.

'Back on *Implacable*, the radar watch had seen the second blip disappear from the screen, and the return of only one Avenger confirmed their fears that a aircraft had ditched. The destroyers screening the Fleet were instructed to keep a sharp lookout for distress signals and, in fact, one of our rockets was seen from almost fifty miles away. Shortly after firing our third rocket, the destroyer HMS *Teaser* picked us up and later that day we rejoined our carrier via the breeches-buoy, little the worse for our experience. We participated, without further incident, in Operation INMATE, the attack on Truk, just a week later.'

On June 12, TG 111.2 sailed for Truk, arriving at the flying-off point, some 80 miles to the south-west, at dawn on the 14th. Weather was stormy but strikes were launched throughout the day; Avengers with bombs, Fireflies with rockets, and Seafires as fighter-bombers attacked shipping, harbour installations and docks but targets were scarce following the destructive pounding Truk had received from the US Task Forces over the months. One Seafire was shot down by flak and one Avenger ditched. At night, 828 Avengers repeated their bombing tactics of a week earlier, attacking by the light of flares.

On the following day, at dawn, a bombardment of targets ashore was undertaken by the accompanying cruisers and destroyers, with CAPs flown by the carriers, including *Ruler* which had provided a useful back-up for *Implacable*. With the withdrawal of the bombardment force during the morning, further strikes were launched throughout the remainder of the day. Early on the 16th, the TG sailed for Manus, reaching there the next day, where it awaited the arrival of the BPF or Task Force 37 as it was now designated.

* * * *

On June 28, TF 37 sailed from Sydney, leaving behind *Indomitable*, undergoing a refit, and *Indefatigable* requiring urgent repairs. Arriving at Manus on July 4, the TF was joined by *Implacable* and the other ships which had remained there for their repairs and replenishment. After two days, the TF set forth, only to have *Implacable* signal a fault in one of her propulsion units but, owing to the deadline for meeting with the US Third Fleet on the 16th, it was decided to effect repairs with the ship under way. The task was completed the day before the rendezvous - a remarkable achievement by the *Implacable*'s engineering staff.

TF 37 reached the US fleet as it was refuelling, thus providing for the British fleet an unforgettable sight of the awesome size of their allies' naval might. Soon after arrival, Admiral Rawlings reported to his new fleet commander, Admiral Halsey, and it was agreed that the BPF should operate as a task group of the US Third Fleet even though, for political reasons, it would be considered to be operating independently at sixty miles distance. In practice, this put the BPF on the right of the line with the US task groups, a distance of 60 miles across the whole fleet. The coming conflict was to be a preliminary stage in the invasion of the Japanese homelands planned for later in the year. The actions would comprise strikes against enemy air forces and strategic targets on the mainland, destruction of the remaining Japanese Navy and shipping, and the testing of enemy defences in the northern part of the islands. To this end, the Third Fleet had started operations early in July.

In the afternoon, the Third Fleet, including TF 37 as one of its four task groups, sailed eastward to its flying-off position for attacks on airfields and shipping north of Tokyo. At dawn on the 17th, the first attack by British aircraft on the Japanese homeland was launched when Ramrods of Corsairs and Fireflies bombed and strafed airfields. Three Corsairs were hit by flak and ditched but their pilots were subsequently picked up by destroyers. Bad weather then intervened and the next two Ramrods had to be cancelled but, later in the morning, two Ramrods were launched for attacks on a west coast airfield. In the afternoon, *King George V* with two destroyers joined US ships for the night bombardment of industrial targets on the east coast. The next day, despite poor weather conditions initially, strikes were launched around midday; the US target was the battleship *Nagato*, but TF 37 was not permitted to join in these attacks as the Americans considered the destruction of the Japanese navy was their own particular task and not to be shared with others. The British targets were airfields and installations in the Tokyo area, and Ramrods were launched by all three carriers during the day. Thirty enemy aircraft were destroyed or damaged, but two Corsairs from *Formidable* failed to return. The next day, the bad weather persisted and offensive operations had to cancelled, the fleets withdrawing for refuelling until the 22nd. On the 20th, TF 37 met with its Logistics Group, which included *Indefatigable* and three destroyers, which meant that the fleet was up to full strength again. The problem of refuelling continued to bedevil the fleet, both as to the quantity of fuel required and the speed of actual refuelling, the tankers not being up to the task required of them. On this occasion, the shortage of fuel necessitated asking the Americans to refuel three British cruisers - not an easy request to make. Refuelling completed, the fleets set sail for the next series of raids starting on the 24th.

For the Americans, the target was to be the Naval base at Kure, where remnants of the Japanese Navy were lying up, while the British were allocated airfields and shipping as their targets. During the day, over 400 sorties were flown for the loss of four aircraft. For the first time since Sakishima, Avengers were in action, flying five combined strikes; one of these was on Tokushima, a medium-bomber airfield strongly defended with 200 anti-aircraft guns. Gordon Passmore, a TAG serving with 828, was on the raid and his vivid description of the action is based on his contemporary notes. The strike force comprised 20 Avengers, 12 from *Implacable* and 8 from *Formidable*, escorted by 8 Fireflies, 12 Seafires and 4 Corsairs.

'When we took off, at 0600, weather conditions were poor and we climbed steadily to get above the cloud which decreased as we approached the coast. The clearing skies enabled us to reduce height to avoid detection by the enemy radar. Landfall was made without incident and, looking down upon the scene below, I immediately thought of Scotland - yet, at the same time, it was so different. The sky was so beautifully blue and seemed to extend to infinity, whilst the small smudges of cloud looked like patches of melting snow, with the sea below a clear dark blue. The whole picture was so utterly peaceful and idyllic but I was brought back to reality with a jolt by an excited Jap voice coming up on our radio frequency. Immediately after, the pilot exclaimed, "Hell, this is it!' and he was right, the sky seemed to be filled with bursting shells but, fortunately for us, concentrated between the two Avenger squadrons. The accuracy of the flak was uncanny and I lost no time in climbing out of the turret to the rear cabin where I proceeded to drop bundles of "rope" (metallic strip for distorting enemy radar) through the flare tube. After a short time, the flak subsided, for whatever reason, and the respite allowed us to peel off and commence our dive. On the way down, it was not possible to see much from the turret apart from the aircraft behind and the flak bursts. Suddenly, the aircraft was shaken by a tremendous concussion followed by violent peppering against the fuselage. My instant conclusion was that we had been hit by flak but soon after, the aircraft was shaken by even more violent buffeting and I realised that we had been hit by blast and debris from the first wave of Avengers. We completed our dive and made our exit flying low over the mud flats. The sight was quite chaotic, debris from aircraft, vehicles, hangars, and buildings flying around - just like a bad American movie! Despite the distractions, I was still able to use the turret gun to advantage, getting in some good bursts at a couple of twin-engined bombers and at the AA guns on our way to the rendezvous.

'A brief interlude of relative calm was interrupted by an abrupt message over the R/T: "Hawk gone down in flames," followed almost instantly by my pilot shouting over the intercom, "It rolled over on its back and went straight in." We circled the spot but the only thing remaining was an uninflated dinghy. The other Avengers soon arrived and we quickly formed up and set course for the "guard" destroyer some 50 miles away. I then got down into the rear cabin to check the bomb-bay, via the perspex panel in the cabin floor, and to my horror saw a 500lb bomb rolling around. After a hurried word with the pilot, I obtained permission from the flight leader to leave the formation to jettison the bomb, which we managed to do at the first attempt. Then, rejoining the formation, we saw the Seafires of the fleet CAP bearing down on us when some 30 miles from the TF. Having been vetted for possible Jap intruders, we were given clearance to continue our approach and it was at this time that the R/T burst into life - our accompanying Seafires were running out of fuel.

'"This is Red Two, only 9 gallons of juice left."

'"Red Four, only 12 gallons."

'"Green Three, I make 15."

'The *Implacable* then broke radio silence.

'"What delay can you accept, Red Two?"
'"Five minutes before I bale out," came the reply.
'Red Four interjected, "I'll make it a duet."
'Reaching *Implacable*, we looked down with disbelief at the deck crowded with aircraft waiting to take off; the question was whether the deck could be cleared before the fighters ran out of fuel. We knew that ditching in an Avenger the crew had a good chance of survival, whereas the Seafire was known to sink like a stone, hence the reference by the pilots to baling out, but to do so in the landing approach was, of course, impossible. The carrier turned into wind and started launching the planes at record speed but the minutes of waiting seemed like hours to us as spectators, so we guessed what the fighter boys were feeling. At last, over the air came the magic words, "Come in Red Two." We watched anxiously as the plane approached the round-down and sighed with relief as it touched down for a perfect landing. One by one, the Seafires landed on without any mishaps and we started breathing again.'

So ended, at 0915, the first Avenger raid on Japan; one Avenger from 848 was lost, the TAG was PO(A) G.C. Rawlinson. Just three hours later, Gordon took off on another raid, this time it was Takamatsu, a heavy bomber airfield in northern Shikoku.

The second combined strike of the day, looking for shipping targets in the Inland Sea, came upon a Kobe Class escort carrier in Shido Wan harbour and, in the subsequent attack, succeeded in making a direct hit on the carrier. Further attacks were made during the day, and Roy Gibbs, TAG serving with 820, was in one of the Avengers; his log book records three hits on the flight deck. In addition to the damage to the carrier, two frigates were sunk and other smaller craft damaged. In total over 400 sorties were flown that day. On the next day, strikes against Tokushima and shipping were continued but because of the worsening weather conditions, strikes planned for the afternoon were cancelled and the fleets withdrew for refuelling. There were a number of attempts by enemy aircraft to close the fleets but these were intercepted and driven off. The most successful of these interceptions was of four torpedo-bombers, by Hellcats from *Formidable*, of which three were shot down and the fourth damaged. Replenishment and refuelling occupied the next two days, then it was back into action off Japan.

July 28 turned out to be the day that the Imperial Japanese Navy ceased to exist as a fighting force; the US Third Fleet sinking two battleships, four cruisers and a number of lesser vessels, with many others damaged. These achievements were considered by the US Commander, Admiral Halsey, as "a smashing victory". Be that as it may, the British Fleet played no part in it but, instead, attacked airfields, shipyards, and shipping in the Inland Sea. In all, 260 sorties were flown against the enemy, including four combined strikes, which met fierce resistance resulting in the loss of eight aircraft. As there were no air strikes planned for the following day, the fleets withdrew in the afternoon.

On the morning of the 29th, *King George V* with three destroyers joined a US bombardment group for the shelling of the industrial area around Hammamatsu, on the south east coast of Honshu. The bombardment, at around 12 miles range, lasted for an hour during which hundreds of shells were fired into the area before the group withdrew at 0030 on the 30th. The air strikes that day were, once again, upon airfields and shipping, 330 sorties being flown for the loss of three fighters and their pilots. A number of light naval units and freighters were attacked, of which several were sunk and others damaged. The fleet withdrew in the evening for a one-day refuelling operation which the British TF was viewing with concern, as it had the greatest difficulty in refuelling even within a two-day period. In the event, a typhoon threatened to pass near the refuelling area so the fleets moved to the south and spent two days refuelling and replenishing.

With the fuelling operation completed on August 2, the fleets were preparing for the next strike day on the 5th, but this date was changed when Admiral Halsey was ordered to withdraw from the planned area of operations; the reason for the order, unknown at the time, was the dropping of the atomic bomb on Hiroshima, scheduled for the 6th. During these few days, the fleets sailed northwards and took the opportunity to refuel and replenish. The carrier air groups, which had not flown for a week, put in some flying training to keep them at peak effectiveness. It was at this time that Gordon Passmore, an 828 TAG, was briefed for a torpedo attack on a heavy cruiser, discovered by photo-reconnaissance in Kure harbour; the strike to be at dawn on the 6th. Gordon did not look forward to the proposed strike and was thankful for the change of plans caused by the Bomb. The actual news of the Hiroshima attack was heard by the fleet on the 7th and was the subject of much discussion at all levels, especially as to its impact upon the ending of the war. In the evening the fleets sailed for their next day flying-off position for strikes on northern Honshu. However, dawn on the 8th revealed foggy conditions which worsened and so all strikes were cancelled and no CAPs were flown.

Early on the 9th, two cruisers and three destroyers joined a US bombardment group for the bombardment of the town of Kamaishi, on the coast of northern Honshu. In the meantime, the carrier air groups were in action after a respite of ten days; for the BPF, the day proved to be its most successful for the number of sorties flown and the results achieved. Four combined strikes, with Avengers, were launched on airfields and shipping; over 60 aircraft were destroyed or damaged while a number of light naval units, including destroyers, torpedo boats, launches, escort vessels and other small craft, were sunk or badly damaged. Losses were the highest for the whole period of operations, including seven fighters and one Avenger, from which two pilots and a TAG were picked up from the sea. One of the Corsair pilots, from *Formidable*, lost that day was Lt. R.H. Gray, RCNVR, who was leading a Ramrod of 8 Corsairs, spotted a destroyer at Onagawa Wan and dived to attack with bombs. Despite heavy fire from ground batteries and ships, which set his aircraft on fire, he pressed home his attack, hitting the destroyer, which was sunk in the explosion. He was subsequently awarded the VC for his courageous action. Gordon Passmore, 828 TAG, who took part in a strike on shipping at Onagawa Wan on that day, witnessed the attack by Lt. Gray but not realising, at the time, the identity of the pilot. During the day, news of the dropping of the second atomic bomb was received, this time on the city of Nagasaki in Kyushu. The news increased the speculation regarding the possible ending of the war within the next few weeks or even days.

Admiral Halsey signalled the fleets that strikes would continue on the 10th, 12th and 13th August, with refuelling to take place on the 11th. This operational requirement created a dilemma for Admiral Rawlings, who had arranged to withdraw TF 37 after the 10th to refit and replenish in Sydney, in readiness for its participation in Operation OLYMPIC, the landings in Kyushu planned for November. Nevertheless, he offered to stay until the 12th, when shortage of fuel would, of itself, necessitate withdrawal. On the 10th, strikes were launched against airfields and shipping, resulting in over 50 aircraft destroyed or damaged and several naval and merchant vessels damaged. In a combined attack on Koriyama airfield, four aircraft were lost, including an Avenger from 828 Squadron, whose crew survived the crash but was captured and imprisoned. Fortunately, although badly treated, their confinement was short and they lived to tell the tale; the TAG was PO(A) Jack Rogerson. The fleets then withdrew and that evening the first announcement of the possibility of the Japanese accepting the surrender terms came from a Tokyo news agency. Early the next day, refuelling began in readiness for the strikes on the 12th, but warning of an approaching typhoon led to the cancellation of the day's programme. So it was that, on the 12th, most of the BPF sailed for Sydney, via Manus. For those leaving, the disappointment of not being present at the final surrender of an implacable enemy was offset by the prospect of an early return home. At least, a token British force was staying behind to join the US Navy in the occupation of Japan. The force, designated TG 38.5, consisted of *King George V, Indefatigable,* two cruisers and ten destroyers.

On the 13th, with the surrender position still unresolved, Admiral Halsey ordered strikes to be launched. A morning strike was flown off by *Indefatigable* for an attack on a chemical factory at Onagawa but a second strike had to be cancelled because of weather conditions over the targets. During the day, enemy attacks on the fleets increased and 21 aircraft were shot down. TG 38.5 refuelled from US tankers on the 14th and, at dawn the next day, *Indefatigable* launched its last strike of the war with six Avengers, four Fireflies and eight Seafires. On the way to the targets, of airfields and factories, the strike force was intercepted by Zeke fighters of which four were shot down and others damaged. In the strikes, an Avenger and a Seafire were lost to flak but the crew of the former survived. Later in the morning, news of the Japanese acceptance of the peace terms was received and offensive operations came to an end. Nevertheless, shortly after this news, an enemy aircraft managed to drop two bombs near the *Indefatigable* before being shot down by Corsairs. In fact, two more enemy aircraft were shot down by CAPs over the next few hours. Roy Gibbs, a TAG on 820 Squadron, recalls that,

> 'We "spliced the mainbrace" and those who had saved up their tots, for such an occasion, lost no time in bringing them out to celebrate. We thought that the last strike had been unnecessary and had led to needless losses of men and aircraft.'

TG 37 had, in the eight strike days over Japan, flown 1600 offensive sorties, during which they had destroyed or damaged 347 enemy aircraft and over 350,000 tons of enemy shipping; operational losses of aircraft had been 141, including replacements for those damaged, in which 32 aircrew had been killed or were missing. The statistics showed that, when compared with those of its American Allies, the BPF had "fought its corner" remarkably well, considering the replenishment difficulties under which it had operated.

* * * *

On August 16, the *Duke of York* joined TG 38.5 as the flagship with Admiral Fraser, Commander-in-Chief of British Pacific Fleet, aboard. Then the TG met their Support Group for a three-day replenishment period during which CVE *Speaker* brought replacement aircraft for the *Indefatigable* and CVE *Ruler* while preparations were completed for the British contingent which was to form part of the landing forces. However, owing to the presence of typhoons in the area, entry into Japanese waters was delayed but, finally, on the 27th, the first Allied ships anchored in Sagami Wan and from there entered Tokyo Bay which, by the end of the month, contained nearly 200 ships. On September 2, the formal ceremony of the signing of the surrender documents was performed on board USS *Missouri*, General MacArthur signing on behalf of the Allied Powers and amongst other signatories was Admiral Fraser for Great Britain.

During this period, *Indefatigable* had remained at sea and had spent the time searching for POW camps, the location of which were mostly unknown to the Red Cross. As a result, aerial searches were introduced and many camps were discovered in this way. Aircraft from *Indefatigable*, took part in these reconnaissances and were successful in finding one at Yokkaichi, on the coast south of Nagoya. It was decided to drop supplies to the prisoners and, following a request to the ship's company, sufficient quantities of foodstuffs, cigarettes, sweets, and personal gifts were collected which, together with medical supplies from the Sick-bay, filled fifteen large canvas kitbags. These, fitted with parachutes, were loaded into the bomb-bays of a flight of 820 Squadron Avengers. TAG, Bill Jones, was in one of the aircraft making the drop.

'The flight, that morning, was a relaxed affair, the skies completely empty of enemy aircraft and no flak awaiting our arrival over the target. As we crossed the shoreline, I saw the prison camp below - a compound, close to the water's edge, with wooden huts, some painted with the letters PW on the roofs. On the sandy shore, outside the compound, a group of scantily-clad figures stared up at us, waving frantically as if we had been expected. Marked out on the sand was the message "Yanks 196 BR 25 DU 75", presumably referring to the nationality of the prisoners in the camp.

'We circled the camp before swinging out to sea to make a long level approach to drop our cargo then breaking off, in a wide arc, to watch the parachutes descend. Not all of them landed in the compound, some fell short into the sea, while others overshot falling outside the compound. All the time, the figures on the beach remained looking up and waving as if afraid to look away lest we disappear; so near to freedom and yet so far. We continued to circle, equally spellbound, until, reluctantly, we had to reform and make our way back to *Indefatigable*; the excitement generated by our mission slowly ebbing away. On our return, we found that we had missed the opportunity of taking part in a mass flight of the Third Fleet's aircraft over Tokyo but, for me, nothing could equal the memory of that excited group of figures on the beach at Yokkaichi; it is one that has stayed with me to this day.'

The supply drop had included a brief message of encouragement to the prisoners from *Indefatigable* plus personal messages from members of the ship's company including one from Bill Jones's observer, S/Lt Johnny Walker, who received a reply while in Tokyo Bay. L/Cpl. G. Rochester was the writer of the letter from which the following extracts are taken:

Dear John,
I wish to thank you and all on board for everything you have done for us in the last few days. The first day we saw the British Navy overhead we went absolutely mad, and we were scared in case you missed us.
You men have no idea how we felt when we knew that the Navy was here, because we have been looking for you for the last three and a half years, but we always knew that someday you would win the war.
The food you gave us has done wonders for everyone. We are all looking much better so we shall be fit and well by the time we reach 'Good old England', which we hope will be very soon ......
I have more letters to write so I will close wishing you and the ship all the best.

Indefatigable received another letter some time later from the Senior Officer at Yokkaichi P.O.W. Camp, Major Donald G. Thompson, US Army Reserve. Extracts from his letter are given below:

> *It is beyond my ability as a writer to express the heartfelt thanks which my men and myself feel toward the men aboard your ship. The wonderful spirit which they showed in gathering up all the many food, clothing, and tobacco items from their own personal supplies and messes is what makes life really worthwhile. Especially after having spent three and a half years under the Japs!*
> *There were many, many tears shed that first day when your Avengers came over our camp and dropped the supplies - I know when I read your note I dropped a tear or so too - from nothing more than happiness!*
> *Everything which you and your men dropped to us was recovered, even those which dropped in the bay - we saved all - the personal items which the men sent were truly wonderful and all of us there were mighty thankful for everything.*
> *I wish too, to thank your medical men especially for getting the sulpha drugs to us - we had an American Staff Sergeant who had been hit, July 30th, with a 50 cal. explosive bullet in the legs. Both feet had to be amputated. By the time your men arrived over the camp, there was much infection forming on both legs, but thanks to the good old HMS Indefatigable and her men, my American Sergeant went aboard the USS Rescue Hospital Ship with no infection at all, and in good physical condition, everything considered!*

Finally, the *Indefatigable* sailed into Tokyo Bay on September 5 but soon left for Sydney. The ship was by now very short of supplies, especially foodstuffs and such minor luxuries as cigarettes and

chocolate, but as Roy Gibbs commented,
> 'With some crafty scrounging from the Americans, we obtained enough supplies for a well-rationed return to Sydney.'

Arriving in Sydney on September 18, 820 Squadron flew ashore to Nowra where it reduced to 12 aircraft. Many aircrew, some of whom had been engaged on continuous operations against the Japanese for eight months, were drafted home on troopships. The squadron remained ashore in Australia, apart from a month's trip to New Zealand on *Indefatigable*, until the end of January, 1946. Then, it re-embarked on *Indefatigable* for the UK, where it was disbanded on March 16.

* * * *

When the BPF sailed from Sydney in June, *Indomitable* was left behind to enter dry-dock for repairs to her propeller shaft necessitated by the kamikaze attacks during the Sakishima operations. For this period, 857 was ashore at Nowra but, on August 2, it was due to fly aboard. Chief TAG, Bill Pirie, flying with the squadron CO, was the first to land.

> 'When the *Indomitable* came through the heads at Sydney, the waves were extremely high, with the odd one breaking over the flight deck. As we approached the round-down, the stern of the ship rose sharply, with the result that we missed all the arrester wires and slid up the deck. The wing hit the armour-plate around the Bofors gun and the wing slowly crumpled up like a concertina, or so it seemed at the time. Luckily, no one was injured in our crash but it meant that further landings had to be cancelled for the time.'

In early August, the BPF was reinforced by the battleship *Anson*, the 11th Aircraft Carrier Squadron of four light fleet carriers, the 2nd Cruiser Squadron and a number of destroyers. The most important tasks facing the British Command was the evacuation of POWs and the re-occupation of Commonwealth territories, particularly Hong

Kong. On the 15th, Admiral Harcourt, in *Indomitable* sailed with his Task Group, arriving off Hong Kong on the 29th. There he transferred his flag to the cruiser *Swiftsure* and, accompanied by an escort including mine-sweepers, entered the harbour as the new Commander in Chief of the Crown Colony. The *Indomitable* remained at sea to police the operation in case of any Japanese attempts to attack the fleet. In the event, three enemy light craft were spotted putting to sea and were intercepted by 857 Avengers; Bill Pirie was in the lead aircraft.

> 'We dived on the boats trying to get them to turn back but to no avail, then we tried some bursts of 0.5 machine-gun fire but they still continued on course, so our ultimate deterrent had to be used - bombs. In the ensuing attacks all three boats were sunk.'

Later, the remainder of the suicide boats were destroyed at their moorings, and by September 1, all enemy forces had been expelled from the island. The squadron flew ashore to Kai Tak, the Hong Kong airport where a Mobile Naval Air Base was set up.

At the end of the month, 857 re-embarked on *Indomitable*, sailing to Sydney, where it flew ashore to Nowra on October 11, but the squadron was approaching the end of the road. Leaving its aircraft ashore, 857 boarded *Indomitable* for passage to the UK where, on November 30, it disbanded.

* * * *

In the meantime, the three carriers, which sailed for Australia on August 12 with the rest of the BPF, had arrived at Sydney where the three squadrons of Avengers flew ashore. In the cases of 848 and 849, after a few weeks, they embarked on *Victorious* for passage to the UK, leaving their aircraft behind. On arrival, October 31, both squadrons were disbanded.

In the case of 828, on *Implacable*, it was to be the last of the Avenger squadrons to be disbanded. TAG, Gordon Passmore, remembers the trip to Sydney when the ship called in at Manus where *Implacable*, "dressed overall", held a most impressive Thanksgiving

Service. During the short stay there, he was surprised to have a visit from his brother who was serving on the submarine depot ship *Resource* which happened to be at Manus that day. The brothers had not met for two years and, as it turned out, they would not meet for another 21 years.

Gordon has also described the day-to-day life on *Implacable* during its time in the Pacific. The ship was operating with nearly 80 aircraft, well above its normal complement, and these extra squadron personnel together with the Admiral's staff and the US liaison staff, meant that overcrowding was inevitable. As a result, living conditions, especially in the hot humid climate, were both debilitating and irksome. In the TAGs' mess, conditions were so congested that, at night, hammocks were slung "wall to wall", with some unfortunates having to sleep under the mess tables or in the gangways - not the best conditions for refreshing sleep. Movement around the ship was very restricted, owing to the water-tight doors having to be kept closed, and TAGs tended to move between their mess and the ready-room in the Island, with visits to the mess-hall and the washrooms. Water for washing was in short supply and available only intermittently which, at times of high humidity, was particularly difficult to live with. Dress of the day was trousers and long-sleeved shirts, which did not help the prickly-heat rash which was rife. At least, there was central messing in the American style, even though the food was not of their standard, a lot of it being dehydrated; the two most inedible of the meals were salted cod and soya sausages. The NAAFI canteen ran out of edible supplies after a short time at sea but did run a "soda fountain" and there were occasional film shows. What was surprising was that for over two months at sea, under such trying conditions, everyone remained even-tempered and there were no ugly incidents which could easily have arisen in such circumstances. The only time when trouble nearly erupted, was on July 4, American Independence Day, when the US personnel aboard were allowed ashore to celebrate. Their boisterous return aboard, did not go down too well with their stone-cold sober mess-mates but, the next day, all was forgiven when the Americans distributed packets of chocolate and other items in short supply. The life-style was not one which was conducive to getting a maximum effort from servicemen engaged in an arduous and bloody conflict but, incredibly, neither did it vitiate their performance.

When the ship arrived at Sydney, the squadron flew ashore to Nowra where it was re-equipped with new Avenger IIIs, which still brings forth the comment from Gordon,

'And to think that we had trained and operated throughout the last seven months with clapped-out Avenger Is with some Avenger II replacements.'

While Gordon and other aircrew were drafted back to the UK, the squadron remained at Nowra until early May, 1946, when, leaving its aircraft behind, it embarked on *Implacable* for the UK, where it disbanded on June 3rd.

Indefatigable she may be, but I'm not.

LOOKING BACK

In the FAA, the wartime role of the Avenger squadrons was restricted to around two and a half years and, of this period, the first eight months of 1945 saw most of the operational action. By the end of 1944, three squadrons had been disbanded, leaving three operating in European waters and nine in the Far East. It is not surprising that the role of the Avenger squadrons was not widely reported when that of the Far Eastern Fleets, the largest of their kind in history, was similarly ignored. The public's attention was understandably concentrated on the European war and, with its ending, the battles being fought on the other side of the world were too remote to capture the flagging interest in this final stage of the war. Furthermore, the Avenger had not been associated with any spectacular feat of arms, as was the Swordfish with such epics as the torpedo attacks on the *Bismarck* and the night attack on the Italian Fleet at Taranto. It was such actions as these which made the Swordfish, and hence the FAA, famous, not the hundreds of other operations which were not headline news.

When it is considered that the fifteen Avenger squadrons, in total, represented only 200 aircraft, a fairly insignificant force in a world war, their achievements were considerable; Atlantic and Russian convoy duties, mine-laying and bombing strikes off Norway, the Channel Operations during the invasion period, trade protection and bombing strikes, including Palembang, in the Indian Ocean, the Sakishima Gunto campaign, and the strikes on mainland Japan. In the course of these actions, TAGs were awarded 26 DSMs and 24 MIDs, while 39 of their number were killed. An indication of the hazardous nature of carrier flying is shown by an analysis of Avenger replacements for the BPF. During the four months of operations, 95 Avengers had to be replaced; of these 22 arose as a result of non-operational damage while 14 were lost with their crews, leaving 59 lost through deck landings, ditchings and other causes - a considerable loss factor for six squadrons, with a complement of around 90 aircraft. It says something for the resolution of the crews and the sturdiness of the Avenger which ensured that they lived to fly another day.

With the surrender of Japan, the role of the Avenger squadrons came quickly to an end and by November, 1945, just two were left: 820 and 828. They remained based in Australia, although most of the original aircrew returned to the UK for demobilisation, but both were disbanded over the next six months.

In 1953, one hundred Avenger TBM-3Es, as used by the US Navy, were supplied under the Mutual Defence Assistance Programme; these were used to re-equip two squadrons, 815 and 824, superseding Barracudas and Fireflies respectively. At the end of 1953, eighty Avenger A.S.4 and A.S.5 aircraft, fully modified for British requirements, came into service; the A.S.4s with 820 and 824 Squadrons and the A.S.5s with 814 and 815. In 1955, the Fairey Gannet entered service and replaced the Avengers, which were later used by several of the RNVR Air Divisions until disbanded. Finally, in 1958, 831 Squadron, on reforming for a role in electronic warfare, incorporated a flight of four Avenger A.S.6s which operated until the middle of 1959.

In the United States, nearly 10,000 Avengers were produced in the 12 years of its operational life, the greatest number of any carrier based strike aircraft. Of this total around 1,000 were supplied to the FAA and it is unfortunate that few of the wartime Avengers survived for display in our museums. At the end of the war, some of our carriers, based in Australia, spent months dumping thousands of aircraft, including Avengers, into the sea, off the east coast. The terms of the Lend-Lease Agreement with America was the reason for this action; any aircraft retained would have had to be paid for and, as the USN did not wish to have them returned, then all had to be disposed of. Ironically, in the past few months, reports have been received of the locating of one of the dumping grounds, off the

Queensland coast, north of Brisbane. The report claims that some are undamaged resting on their undercarriages on the sea-bed so, perhaps, after 50 years, some of these historic aircraft can be salvaged even at this late stage.

In those wartime days, sitting in the Avenger's gun-turret looking back, searching the skies, I never imagined that, 50 years hence, I should be looking back, trying to recapture the essence of those times for others to read.

One of ours, he says.

CONTRIBUTORS

A.S.R. Austin

J. Barnes

H.J. Beardshaw

W.A. Beckett

W. B. Campbell

H. Copping

S.A. Crawford

J.K. Gardiner

R.J.W. Gibbs, MID

J.C. Hind

C.S. Hodgkinson

W.J.D. Jones

E.W. Larwood

J.R. Mackenzie

J.G.C. Minards

J. Munro

G.S. Passmore

W.T. Pirie, DSM

G.A. Rock

S.J. Sage

G.W. Smith

A.G. Stocker

P.A. Tipney

845 Squadron TAGs on HMS Empress, March 1945
L to R: Southall, Elliot, Munro, Mason, Fletcher, Wealleans,
Graham, Allen, Townsend and Garnett.

820 Squadron Avenger landing on HMS Indefatigable after
a strike on Miyako.

R.J.W. Gibbs

1st April 1944. Three photographs showing the demise of an Avenger while attempting to land on HMS Tracker during the passage of Convoy JW58 to Kola Inlet, Russia.

Geoff Hearn

Warships assembled in Tokyo Bay for the Japanese surrender in 1945. Seen from HMS Indefatigable, with 820 Squadron Avengers in foreground.

R.J.W. Gibbs

We come to destroy the Japanese only.

KEEP AWAY FROM DANGER!

Avoid Japanese aerodromes, harbours or military works of any kind!

HELP US BY HELPING YOURSELVES!

ايغت بايك ۲ صحابت كامي!
جاغن دكت اورغ جفون اتوفكرجأنڽ!
جأوهكن ديري درفد بهاي!

我們只是為了毀壞日本人而來。
你們須遠離，以免受危險！
不要接近日本飛機場，碼頭，及軍事設備！
援助我們，就是救護你們本身。

இப்பானியரை மட்டுமே அழிக்க நாங்கள் வருகிறோம்.
அபாய்த்திலிருந்து விலகிக்கொள்ளுங்கள்!
இப்பானிய விமானகூடங்கள், துறைமுகங்கள், ராணுவ ஸ்தாளங்க
ள் இவைகளுக்கு பக்கத்தில் நீங்கள் வாவே கூடாது!
உங்களை பாதுகாத்துக்கொள்வதன் மூலம எங்களுக்கு உதவுங்கள்!

SMA/17

Typical leaflet dropped on the occupied territories.

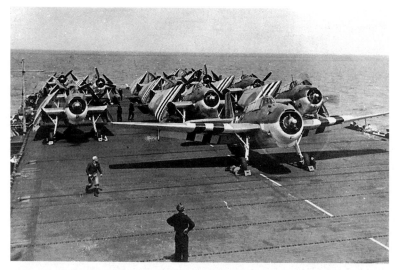

D-Day. S.W. Approaches 846 Squadron on HMS Tracker

FAA Museum

A Mk1 Avenger of 846 Squadron from HMS Ravager,
ditched in Chesapeake Bay.

FAA Museum

832 and 845 Squadron crews being briefed in the Admiral's cabin aboard HMS Illustrious for Surabaya raid, May 1944.
Central Press Photos.

832 Squadron Avengers on the way to Surabaya.
G.W. Smith

845 Squadron Avenger being boosted from HMS Ameer at Trincomalee.

FAA Museum

854 Squadron aircraft goes over the side of HMS Illustrious.

FAA Museum

853 Squadron Avenger aboard HMS Arbiter.

H.J.C.Spencer

853 Squadron Avenger on HMS Tracker at Scapa Flow.

H.J.C.Spencer.

856 Squadron Avenger crash on the round-down of HMS Premier, 30th April 1945 during the last wartime Russian Convoy, JW66.

Stewart Crawford.

*820 Squadron Avenger goes over the side of
HMS Indefatigable during the Sakishima campaign. Alex
Simpson is the TAG climbing aboard in the lower picture.*
R.J.W. Gibbs

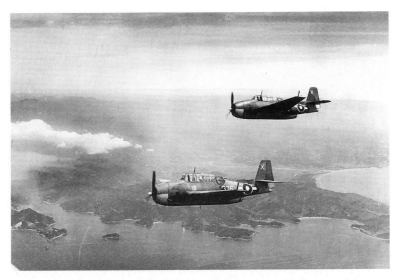

Avengers of 848 Squadron, HMS Formidable in 1945.

FAA Museum.

848 Squadron bombing a Kamikaze base in South Japan, 1945

FAA Museum

Hong
Kong

BURMA

INDIA

Rangoon

Aden

Vishak

Andamans

Cochin

Trincomalee

Colombo
Katukurunda

Sabang

MALAYA

Singapore

Mombasa

Pangkalan Brandan

SUMATRA
Emmahaven

Seychelles

Surabaya

JAVA

MADAGASCAR

Exmouth Gulf

Freemantle

INDIAN OCEAN

PACIFIC OCEAN

Avenger of 849 Squadron, HMS Victorious en-route to Palembang

FAA Museum

Left:
Lt. (A) K.M. Burrenston RNVR
and
S/Lt. (A) W.E. Lintern RNVR.

Right:
Lt. (A) K.M. Burrenston RNVR
and
the author on 12th April 1943

180

Palembang Memorial in FAA Memorial Church, Yeovilton.

HMS Heron

*August 1945, a flight of Avengers from 820 Squadron
dropped supplies to the Prisoner of War Camp at Yokkaichi,
South of Nagoya.*

R.J.W. Gibbs

"Cadjan" hut at RAF Vavuniya.

J.Richardson

SOURCES AND REFERENCES

BAIN, Valerie   *Home On The Range*
                      V. Bain
BEAVER, Paul   *The British Aircraft Carrier*
                      Patrick Stephens Ltd., 1982
BROWN, Eric   *Wings of The Navy*
                      Air Life Publishing Ltd., 1987
BROWN, Eric   *Duels in the Sky*
                      Air Life Publishing Ltd., 1989
BROWN, J.D.   *Carrier Operations in World War II, Royal Navy*
                      Ian Allan 1968
CAMERON, Ian   *Wings of the Morning*
                      Hodder & Stoughton, 1962
FLETCHER, R.G.   *Touch And Go*
                      R.G. Fletcher, 1992
IRELAND, Bernard   *The Rise and Fall of the Aircraft Carrier*
                      Marshall Cavendish Ltd., 1979
JOHNSON, Brian   *Fly Navy*
                      David & Charles, 1981
JUDD, Donald   *Avenger from the Sky*
                      William Kimber, 1985
KEMP, P.K.   *Fleet Air Arm*
                      Herbert Jenkins, 1954
LAMB, Gregor   *Sky Over Scapa, 1939 - 1945*
                      Byrgisey, 1991
POOLMAN, Kenneth   *Illustrious*
                      William Kimber, 1955
POOLMAN, Kenneth   *Escort Carrier 1941 - 1945,*
                      1972
POOLMAN, Kenneth   *The British Sailor*
                      Arms And Armour, 1989
POPHAM, Hugh   *Into Wind*
                      Hamish Hamiton, 1969

RAWLINGS, John D.R.   *Fleet Air Arm*
Ian Allan, 1973

RICHARDSON, N.E.   *The Changi Memorial*
N.E. Richardson

SIMS, Ken   *The Story of the Telegraphist Air Gunners*
TAGA, 1989

SIMS, Ken   *TAGS in Squadrons*
TAGA, 1992

SIMS, Ken   *TAG Awards and "In Memoriam" Lists*
TAGA 1990

SPENCER, H.J.C.   *Ordinary Naval Airmen*
Parapress Ltd., 1994

STURTIVANT, Ray   *The Squadrons of The Fleet Air Arm*
Air Britain Ltd,. 1984

STURTIVANT, Ray   *Fleet Air Arm at War*
Ian Allan, 1982

STURTIVANT, Ray   *British Naval Aviation*
Arms & Armour, 1990

THETFORD, Owen   *British Naval Aircraft Since 1912*
Putnam, 1982

TILLMAN, Barrett   *Avenger at War*
Ian Allan, 1979

WINTON, John   *The Forgotten Fleet*
Michael Joseph Ltd., 1969

WINTON, John   *The War at Sea*
BCA., 1974

WOODMAN, D.W.J.   *H.M.S. Tracker*
Society of Friends of FAA Museum, 1987

GLOSSARY

AA	Anti-aircraft
ADT	Attack Dummy Torpedo
ALT	Attack Like Torpedo
ART	Attack Runner Torpedo
A/S	Anti-submarine
ASV	Air-to-surface vessel radar (British)
BARRACUDA (Fairey)	British carrier dive-bomber
BATSMAN	Deck landing control officer
BEAUFIGHTER (Bristol)	British twin-engined fighter
Bf109 (Messerschmitt)	German fighter
BOGEY	Unidentified aircraft
BOOSTER	Catapult for launching carrier a/c
BPF	British Pacific Fleet
CAP	Combat Air Patrol
C-in-C	Commander-in-Chief
Cdr	Commander
CO	Commanding Officer
CORSAIR (Chance Vought)	US carrier fighter plane
CPO	Chief Petty Officer
CVE	Carrier Vessel Escort
DAUNTLESS (Douglas)	US Carrier dive-bomber
DSM	Distinguished Service Medal
E-boat	German motor torpedo boat
FIREFLY (Fairey)	British fighter-bomber
FAA	Fleet Air Arm
FLAK	Enemy anti-aircraft fire

GALLEY	Cookhouse
GANNET (Fairey)	British carrier bomber
Gp	Group (RAF)
HELLCAT (Grumman)	US carrier fighter
HF	High frequency
HMAS	Her Majesty's Australian Ship
HMCS	Her Majesty's Canadian Ship
HMNZS	Her Majesty's New Zealand Ship
HMS	Her Majesty's Ship
HO	Hostilities only rating
JUDY (Yokosuka)	Japanese Navy dive-bomber
KAMIKAZE	Japanese suicide plane
KNOT	Speed of a nautical mile per hour
L/A	Leading Airman
L/Cdr	Lieutenant Commander
Lt	Lieutenant
MAE WEST	Life jacket
MF	Medium frequency
MID	Mentioned in Dispatches
MV	Motor Vessel
NAAFI	Navy, Army, Air Force Institutes
OSCAR (Nakajima)	Japanese Army fighter
OTU	Operational Training Unit
PO	Petty Officer
PORT	Left side
PR	Photographic Reconnaissance
RAAF	Royal Australian Air Force
RAMROD	Strikes by bombers and fighters on targets of opportunity, within briefed guidelines.
RAF	Royal Air Force
RAN	Royal Australian Navy
RCAF	Royal Canadian Air Force
RCN	Royal Canadian Navy

RDF	Radio Direction Finding
RN	Royal Navy
RNAS	Royal Navy Air Station/Service
RNVR	Royal Naval Volunteer Reserve
ROUND-DOWN	Rounded end of the rear flight deck
RPO	Regulating Petty Officer
R/T	Radio Telephone
SALLY (Mitsubishi)	Japanese Army bomber
SEAFIRE (Supermarine)	British carrier fighter
SORTIE	An operational flight
SPONSON	Projecting gun platform
SS	Steamship
S/Lt	Sub-lieutenant
STARBOARD	Right side
SWORDFISH (Fairey)	British carrier biplane bomber
TAG	Telegraphist Air Gunner
TBR	Torpedo Bomber Reconnaissance
TF	Task Force
TG	Task Group
TOJO (Nakajima)	Japenese Army fighter
U-boat	German submarine
U/S	Unserviceable
USN	United States Navy
USNAS	United States Naval Air Station
USS	United States Ship
VHF	Very high frequency
WILDCAT (Grumman)	US carrier fighter
W/T	Wireless Telegraphy
ZEKE (Mitsubishi)	Japanese Army fighter

INDEX

NOTE. Telegraphist Air Gunners are indicated thus: TAG, irrespective of rank.

Index

189